INVESTED DAD

How to Raise Emotionally Healthy Children and Have Them Become Wildly Wealthy Adults

10 Must-Have Relationships between Parent and Child

6 Activities for Every Developmental Life Stage

3 Phase Method for Exponential Growth

1 Family Legacy to Create

Alfred Gordon Liu

FREE GIFTS

BONUS AUDIOBOOK + WORKBOOK

Congratulations on getting a copy of my book! Get a **Free Copy of the Audiobook and Workbook** created to support the activities in this book and to help my auditory learners as well as busy parents.

For Free Gifts visit: www.InvestedParenting.com

Editing by Andrea McCurry
Photos by Emily Holmes
Artwork by Christina Nguyen
About Author Photo by Phil Planta
Design Concepts by David Capistrano
Developed with Vickie Gould International, LLC
Audiobook ISBN: 9-781777-7311625
Paperback ISBN: 9-781777-731618
E-book ISBN: 9-781777-731601

Visit the author's website at www.alfredgordonliu.com

Table of Contents

Preface

In 2018, just before the first day of Spring, I had the toughest week of my life. And the combination punches that led to my knockdown sounded like this:

> Wednesday - "Sorry, we had to give the job to someone else."
>
> Thursday - "Are you Alfred Liu? You have just been served."
>
> Friday - "Your certification exam results: 87% - FAIL."
>
> Saturday - "Check on your mom, your aunt just passed."
>
> Sunday - "Take me to the hospital now, the baby is coming."
>
> Monday - "Calling because you missed your shift today."
>
> Tuesday - "Daddy, are you coming back home now?"

How much can someone shoulder in one week? Have you ever felt like the world just keeps kicking you when you are down? And you don't have anything else to give, and you are completely exhausted, after years of working so hard, pushing, reaching, and grinding.

Well after that week, I fell hard and far into a deep depression due to the crushing stress I felt as my life seemed to fall apart.

Like many others, working hard was my go-to instrument and my method for building up success. I could count on hard work to manifest anything I wanted. If I just put in the effort, I could make it happen, earn six figures, build my dream house, create a profitable business. Any goal I set for myself through brute force, blind belief, and grunt work, I could manifest it. I mastered a strong mindset, strong work ethic, and always improved my recipe for success.

As I started the new chapter of my life called Parenting, I always knew that I wanted my village of extended family to be close by, probably because both sets of my grandparents lived over ten thousand kilometers away (over 6300 miles). I only met them a handful of times when I was growing up.

So even before my wife and I had our first kids, I devised a beautifully timed, five-year master plan to hustle, grind, and make enough money to construct my dream estate. I dreamed we would live in our urban nine-bedroom, four-bath, corner-lot property, with a newly constructed two-bedroom coach house with an in-law suite at the back. We would also have a nice, shared garden area with a deck separating the two homes, so everyone could gather in harmony and enjoy a nice barbeque as we watched the sunset all together. We would blissfully eat, laugh, and play together. And we when we had our fill, we could each retreat to our corner of the property. It was My One Big Dream and the vision of success in my mind for my perfectly designed life.

But the road to that dream, was not smooth. It was a fight. A fight to balance a corporate training career, real-estate empire, and a growing online retail business, all while freelancing my film production services for extra cash. A fight to oversee construction mishaps, while communicating with inspectors and managing contractors. A fight to withdraw my savings and issue the largest cheques I ever wrote, to reinvest in materializing My One Big Dream. Achieving this dream was a lot to handle and required a lot of energy. No one in my family had ever taken on a project like this before.

I had to man up, take one for the team, and lead the way.

And as I put my head down and dug into the work, five years flew by. My work to build my dream focused me; it narrowed and tunneled my vision.

This work created wonderful blinders that cut everything out that wasn't related to accomplishing the goal, the vision, the mission. But that objective also blinded me to my struggling wife, growing toddler, and aging parents. I couldn't see them or hear their feedback, desires, or wishes. There was no time to check in with their needs. I was a bulldog, holding on to the vision, not looking backwards, and dragging everyone else along for the ride.

I kept saying to myself, "Once construction is done and we get the keys to the property, my dream will all be worth the effort, the heartache, the stress, the suffering. I just gotta get to that One Big Dream moment when I am eating some barbeque and the sun is setting on my face. My family will thank me in the end."

I imagined that One Big Dream sunset barbeque moment was like an Ironman Race finish line. You give the race your all and when you see that ribbon, you just gotta cross it, busting it apart. The sidelines cheer for you and your performance, then a team comes and carries you on their shoulders, as champagne corks pop in the air and you are awarded a medal, like a hero.

But real life wasn't like that at all when I finally crossed the construction finish line and got my keys to my dream estate. There was no ribbon, no celebration, no support team, no champagne, no medal, no appreciation, no thanks. Actually, when I looked up, I found myself all alone at the back of the property, isolated in a newly constructed coach house/ in-law suite that I built for my parents.

I was alone, not because everyone was busy exploring the other sections of the property, but because I had alienated everyone around me. I was so stressed and on edge that people just steered clear of me and avoided any interaction with me for fear that I might snap at them, or they might trigger an outburst. I was wound up so tight that everything that came from my mouth was like fire. Even having crispy chicken versus baked chicken for dinner could set me off.

The dust had barely settled on the new construction floor when I experienced a few breakdowns. From bouts of rage and flaming anger, to fits of uncontrollable, ugly crying, I finally retreated into the soul to numbness, just to navigate my everyday routine responsibilities and duties. I operated like the Walking Dead, roaming and wandering, piecing together the damage I caused along the road to my success and dream.

I had never felt so alone, so broken, so hurt, so betrayed, so wronged, so worthless. I felt like a waste of space and time. And for the first time, I felt like the problem, not the solution or savior I believed I was. I had become the villain in my One Big Dream life story.

I imagined myself as the rage-filled Incredible Hulk who smashed a giant, asteroid-sized crater into the world and left a trail of destruction. As the sun went down and the flames died out, the Hulk transformed into his human form of Bruce Banner, looking back to see the massive damage that his formidable, protective ego caused.

And it was up to this dazed, confused, half-conscious, crushed human to pick up the pieces of a trust-broken marriage, a time-starved child, and his ill and aging parents. Meanwhile all the bystanders had their hearts, trust, thoughts, and opinions trampled on. The damage also extended to innocent siblings and in-laws, who watched a once dependable leader, pillar of connection, and model of togetherness and intimacy, crumble before their eyes in desolation.

They watched me hit rock bottom and as I questioned my own worth in life, I started to liquidate my assets and fold businesses as they cracked, due my lack of focus and the stresses of preparing to fight a court battle that sucked all the mental and emotional capacity that remained. I faltered as I worked to repair my marriage and connect with my own children, while staying in the darkness and doubt of depression. But they stood by as I desperately searched for a new *modus operandi*, a new way of being.

As the leader and the emotional bedrock for our family and friends, our crumbling marriage left our circles of support floundering on how to assist us. No one around us had been in our situation before or could relate fully, so we slipped into silent suffering and cried in desperation. We knew we had to get professional help.

My journey led me to institutional help, everything from employee-assistance programs to clinical counselling. I tried it all, and I spent a few years in group therapy, alongside months of family counselling sessions and weekly visits with medical and psychiatric doctors. All the doctors, professionals, support groups, and medicines helped me set an emotional and mental floor. They became the safety net that kept me from falling further into the abyss of self-harm and prevented me from being a danger to others, as well.

But still this process wasn't enough to bring me out of my pit of despair. I had to couple the institutional help and therapy with visits to personal development specialists and self-help coaches and speakers. I attended the best seminars in transformation.

Recovering my life was an investment as I searched for the right thoughts and life-coaching leaders to walk me out of the dark pit that my own Hulk created. I needed to find someone who had travelled to a similar wasteland as mine to guide me back to new reality and a different way of operating for my breed of both super and broken human. I needed a broken dreamer, entrepreneur, high achiever, doer, manifestor, parent, lover, family person, workaholic, perfectionist, caregiver, leader - in short, a UNICORN.

I was lost after falling from a great height, trying to reach my dreams. Surely something was broken inside of me, and I needed help from others who soared and fell from greater heights than I. I needed to see, hear, and feel other's ginormous falls back to ground zero. And I needed to know that it was possible to survive such a fall. I had to find out how to come back from such a disaster.

No one person had my exact same journey or experience. I had to piece-meal the solution together, to put together a panel of recovery for myself. I had, not just one person, but a team of mentors to put me back together again. I gained my recovery from here and there, putting together my own recipe for resilience.

And I want to share this recipe with you. I have tested the process and have evidence that it works. My ideas and method for recovery can be a roadmap for true wealth. Wealth doesn't just mean money alone, but is complemented by strong mental resilience, deep intimate relationships, lasting emotional fulfillment, rewarding purpose, and greater significance with your own circles. This is what I mean by true wealth in mind, body, and spirit.

The dream home, the businesses, and the assets were easy to fix, rebuild, and manage. The deep childhood re-programming and emotional healing and processing (not just coping) took the most work for me. The marriage, the relationships, the self-identity, reflection, and healthy, mindful habits is where the true investment was. And I wish to guide you so that you may have an easier time than I.

Today, I am 35 pounds lighter, 35 times happier, have less than 35 items on my to-do list every week. And to top it off, I am retired, waking up to workouts, feeding my mind positive messages, and surrounding my heart with great people. I continue that health habit with reading and making investing decisions during market hours. Then I spend my time with my family after hours. I am free from the stress and uncertainty of the rat race, and I'm off the hedonistic treadmill of success.

My struggles led me to find my own self-worth, and they also helped me value other investments as well, like businesses, stocks, and power of the options markets. Detached from the mob mentality, I am truly retired from economic pressures and have the time to invest my energy on what truly matters.

This new way of being has survived my Hulk episode, a global pandemic, and the stress test of an ongoing mental health crisis. It is my time to light my small candle in this world of darkness, to show another way out of the pit of global despair.

As you journey closer to me and enter my circle of influence, know that there is light, there is hope, and there is a way:

- To repair broken relationships with yourself and others.
- To relate and build a healthy relationship with your child.
- To build awareness, strength, and resiliency.
- To heal your deepest scars and release the past.
- To be a leader for your family and community.
- To influence and impact the next generation's future.
- To pass on your wisdom and efforts.
- To ensure your final wishes are fulfilled.

Join me in this venture to see if my path fits you. And if you like where it can take you, I'll see you along the journey. Happy trails.

Acknowledgements

To my wife, Marie, thank you for sticking with me. We were a summer fling that has survived ten cold winters. I am so thankful to have a patient and understanding partner who is willing to accompany me on all my life's seasons. "You and Me" create my favorite pair.

To my children, Catalina and Kaydence, thank you for teaching me how to be a better father, man, and investor. I want you to know that you two will always be my favorite investment and my most valuable assets that I ever have the privilege of caring for.

To my girls' grandparents, John and Ann Liu, as well as Ofelia and Liberato Reyes, thank you for raisin Marie and myself, and showing us what nearly 100 years of marriage looks like. And most importantly, thank you for loving on our two girls and being an active part of their lives on a daily basis. We love seeing your personalities live on in them.

Thank you Dr. John Taveres and Dr. Khanh Nguyen for your professional and medical support. You both cared for me and carried me when I was not strong enough to do it for myself.

To Daddy and Daughter investing mentors, Phil and Danielle Town, thank you for teaching me the Rule1 way of investing and showing me a model of a healthy parent/ adult-child relationship. Both lessons are legacies that my family will carry on and practice for generations.

To the mother and son life-coaching team, Lisa and Jelani Nicholas, thank you for beautifully and vulnerably sharing your personal, business, and family struggles with me. And most importantly, thank you for giving me tools for self-love and self-care and for showing me how to create a safe place for me and my girls to share.

To friends and roomies, Vicky and Bryan Walls, from the Brix Family Farm www.brixfamilyfarm.ca, thank you for being supportive, lifelong friends and for giving me a corner of your farm to rest, reflect, and recharge while I wrote this book.

To St. Mary's Parish Digital Ministry and Faith Community, thank you for nurturing a seed that was planted long ago. I've strayed and it's taken a global pandemic for me to come back and see all the fruits of the garden.

For my baby niece Ava, I first intended this book to be a guide for your dad, including tips and tricks for fathers raising daughters after me. But while writing during the Great Lockdown, I realized my story cannot be just for your dad. I needed to encourage everyone who is struggling and learning.

And so, I write for all the dads who wish to protect and prosper their most valuable assets and who need a little reminder of the light within all the darkness that looms over us during this global pandemic.

Introduction

How can being a better father make me a better investor? And how can being an investor make me a better father? While the worlds of parenting and the stock market may seem so far apart, I found the sweet spot where they benefit, complement, and support each other.

As the parent of two young girls, at six and three-years old, I've often been applauded by the new moms and grandparents who see me bringing my girls to school or those who notice a dad engaged in the parent and tot classes. They often asked me three questions:

1) What do you do?
2) Do you have the day off?
3) What is your secret for being a good Dad?

My typical answer was that I finished work for the day. As an investor living on the West Coast in Pacific Standard Time, the stock market usually opens on Monday to Friday from at 6:30 am and the trading day closes right after lunch.

These were perfect hours for any parents who know or remember the pains of drop-off and pick-up responsibilities while managing a 9-to-5 job or ever-changing shift work. Or if you are contractor, freelancer, business owner, or landlord, how many hours are you chained to your work? How much flexibility do you have to up and leave work, in order to give your children the attention they need?

Just a few years ago, an investor showed me 15 minutes of his working day, and I was amazed how he turned that into $15K. He made $1000 per minute of work, and that was with him explaining his process to me. Now, I teach hundreds of students every month the exact same strategies, techniques, and tools to change their financial futures.

And even though I teach others how to invest, I am also the student, always learning. And I am so grateful for the financial lessons I own now, like how to earn a two-week paycheck in less than two hours of work. I don't need to work harder, longer, or more often to make more money.

Most days, I balance setting up my trades as my kids eat breakfast or brush their teeth. And while they are at school or in class, I get to focus on investment research, earning calls, company valuations, and technical charting while waiting on orders to fill. After lunch, I conduct all my meetings, writing, coaching sessions, and appointments so by 3 pm, I can welcome my children home and continue my dad-on-duty shift, with after-school activities and homework. Or I can just be the fun dad and love on them, be present, snuggle with them, or even go on an impromptu adventure outside.

But something else unexpected happened on the way to achieving financial freedom and accidentally hitting retirement. What would I do with all this energy, work ethic, and hustle muscle that I developed over the years? Where would I spend my time and effort?

At first, I threw my efforts at my investing practice, going deeper in the research, looking at companies and what made them kick. What was their core business? Did I support what they are doing? How did they stay competitive? How were they managed and led? What was their growth forecast? Where do they spend and allocate their dollars? And how did their financials look quarter after quarter?

I must have filtered and studied a few hundred publicly traded companies, in-depth case study after case study, that affixed these investment lenses and goggles to my head. I began to evaluate everything I interacted with by an investor's eye.

Who was the Chief Executive Officer of my family? What did our family stand for and what was our mission statement? What did I want my children to accomplish? What did returns did I want to see from my kids? How was I building them up to be resilient and competitive? Who was on the board of directors that guided them?

Through my investor lens, I started to see how I could take the best leadership practices from Fortune 500 companies and implement them at home with my own kids. I realized my methods as an investor translated well into being a great parent. Both arenas inherently come with a load of responsibility, require a long-term commitment and strategy, develop a keen eye for recognizing value and growth opportunities, and with active management and involvement, can be extremely rewarding.

New dads primarily focus on providing food and shelter for their children. And yes, these basic needs are important for keeping your offspring alive and safe. But I want to introduce you to roles other than the provider and protector, that ensure you invest in your future and nurture your most precious assets, your children, as a part of your investment portfolio.

But it's the last question that people ask when I pick up my kids from school that I really want this book to focus on. "What's my secret?"

I usually can escape answering this question because people focus on "what" I do and "how" I do it. But it is the "why" that is my secret. I just do what is important to me to actively nurture the talents of my children and create a safe and encouraging place to get them back on their own two feet. It's a simple mission. I'm good at what I do because of this one simple secret: I care.

And that caring, that concern, attentiveness, and vested interest is the hardest part to develop and grow. Developing this area may be the one thing I cannot give you or teach you. *How* do you care about your little ones?

I can show you the benefits of caring and open your eyes a bit, but you are the one who has to want it. You must have that seed of care in you. If your desire to nurture and develop isn't there or is not ready yet, come back to this book later, when the time is right.

But if you are open to caring, skip to the latter chapters to see the stories from greats before us and how they left a legacy of wealth and still impact others beyond the grave. Learn their tips and tricks on how they nurtured their children and ensured their wealth and work would carry on for generations.

What I really came to understand as an investor is how to determine the true value of an investment, not just its price.

For the past year, we faced a global pandemic which left many without a job, without income, without certainty, without choices, and without a community. And for that reason, I want this book to keep you company, to be with you, like a lifelong friend grabbing a drink, going on a walk, or sitting around the kitchen counter having a great chat. This book is an uplifting reminder of the things that are important to us, and the gentle rekindling and encouragement to invest more deeply through all the stages of a child's growth. And I promise the real returns will exceed your expectations if done with just a few of the tips and methods outlined in the following chapters.

Let's dive in and help you become a better dad with some tips borrowed from the investing world.

The 3-PAIR Method

This book's chapters are structured from my one core concepts taken from my coaching programs called the 3-Pair Method (3PM). The 3PM simply focuses on one child and parent relationship (PAIR) and helps you identify what you need to let go of (PARE) and what space you need to clear for what you need to grow (PEAR), nurture, and desire.

The pear fruit tree was chosen as a symbol for the 3 Pairs Method, to help remind my clients (and myself) that we can't force growth or will healing to happen. It comes organically.

We need to approach our lives and our own development like growing a real tree. The fruit will only grow and appear if the conditions are right, if planted in fertile soil, with lots of sunshine, water, and help to fend off pests and disease.

For my clients, the "tree" represents an area of life that they want to work on, like the relationship tree, the career tree, and in this book, the parenting and the investing tree.

And the fruit, "the pear," represents the goal, the result, and the outcomes. These goals may include a relationship goal such as going to the next level with your life partner, or a career outcome like making a successful transition to a new field, or a personal aim like how to find my identity as a new parent.

We all have several trees, with the dreams and wishes they represent in our lives, that were planted a long time ago. As our priorities and attention shifted over the years, some of those trees have grown unattended and untamed. But some of us are lucky enough to find an open meadow where we are free to plant some new seeds.

The pear fruit is a metaphor and reminder that we can only nurture the tree, provide the right conditions for it to grow and flourish, and in turn, produce fruit. The fruit of our labour is our desired outcome and results.

The opposite is true as well. We can't just be a passive bystander when it comes to the trees that rooted deep in our past or even ones planted by our well-intentioned parents. If we leave these trees unattended and untamed, they will grow and flourish to the detriment of everything else.

All personal life-coaching and self-development work are usually two-fold. One part addresses the physical or material aspects of our lives, like weight loss, monetary goals, or habitual behaviours. These represent the low-hanging fruit and branches we can usually see or easily identify. While we can pick, prune, or address the surface issues, they usually stem from or are rooted in something much deeper.

The second part of personal growth work looks at what is beneath the surface. How did this habit form? Where did this idea or seed come from? And what supports and nurtures this behaviour?

In my experience, whether the fruit is a juicy, healthy marriage, a prickly personality, or a habit of self-sabotage, the reason that it shows up is because that fruit is nourished by something deep below. The roots sap a powerful and emotional memory or a traumatic childhood experience that continually feeds and supports the roots, trunk, and branches, nourishing its environment. This environment includes the crap and dirt the habit is rooted in, and the air, the sun, and the rain that surrounds it.

Most of the world's trees are in the wild, with Mother Nature providing at a distance. But the trees that are in the care of a farmer, gardener, or an arborist tend to flourish and grow stronger, producing more fruit. The human and tree **pair** is an unusual pairing in nature. But the tree can grow healthier and stronger with the human protection. And the human can be nourished by the clean air and fruit that the tree produces. The **PAIR Method** only works if a relationship is created that is both harmoniously interdependent and mutually beneficial over its lifecycle.

From the beginning, the caregiver of the tree works alongside Mother Nature to ensure the seed of the tree has a great head start by ensuring the ground it is planted in is nutrient rich, and the soil is firm enough with good drainage, so it doesn't drown. When the windy season comes, the gardener stakes and supports the young trunk to withstand the forces and elements.

And as this young, growing tree reaches for the skies, its arms are pruned, cut, and trimmed back in a way so that the branches get enough space to grow and capture the sun's light. This idea brings us to the importance of the **PARE Method**. Most of us parents know that cutting out sugar and processed foods is good for your child's growth. So is cutting out negative influences such as ignorant celebrities or public figures. As much as we want to give our children everything and anything they desire, it is usually this paring method to cut out negative influences that helps promote a firmer, healthier foundation to support the rest of the tree.

When you start to see the results from your influence, your impact, and your discipline, your desired outcome will start to bud and come into fruition, just like when you reinforce manners like saying, "please and thank you," or establishing a routine of homework or mediation. In this book I relate these outcomes as the fruit, the PEAR.

The **PEAR Method** focuses on how to actively grow and nurture a bud when you see it first develop. These are usually spotted on the branches, and some of the buds will flower and turn into fruit.

It is up to the human in this pair to recognize what the tree needs and when it is a season for the flowers to bloom.

We must isolate and concentrate our energies on producing the desired fruits. As farmers, gardeners, or parents, we know we must protect that growth or unripened fruit from pests and disease for it to develop fully.

Now many species of plants reproduce, giving birth to hundreds or sometimes thousands of offspring so that a few may survive. We humans can typically only produce one offspring in a single year. So, unlike a tree or other species which produces many babies at once, we must employ a strategy to focus our attention on growth and development to ensure our child not just survives but thrives.

In this book, the 3-Pair Method is specifically applied to the ten growth phases of the human development in our human life cycle. Each chapter focuses on the importance, impact, and benefits of specific parent-child relationship pairing. For each **pair,** we will dive into what habits, behaviours, and beliefs can be **pare**d (cut/ removed/ pruned) from our lives and which ones we can **pear** (grow/ nurture/ develop).

The strategies and concepts of the 3PM are colored with examples from the investing world which deepens and draws parallels to the importance of each parent-child relationship pair. This method also portrays how healthy parental views can help promote solid growth of wealth, and not just the monetary definition of success.

About the 3-PARE / 3-PEAR Chapter Challenges

As an author and coach, I don't want you just to read my thoughts, words, and lessons then put them on a shelf. I want you to take action by trying out the methods that work for me so we can celebrate your success story too!

Within each chapter, a section is dedicated to providing three challenges that help you remove, cut, and pare something out of your life called the **3-PARE Challenges**.

As well as removing or cutting out something, each chapter has a section where growth, nurturing, or protecting the fruits of your efforts are in focus. These **3-PEAR Challenges** are activities that will often produce surprising and insightful results. They are designed for you push past the comfort zone and move you into the growth zone.

About the 3-PAIR Takeaway Messages

The 3-Pair Takeaway sections summarize the key points for each chapter. I know how valuable time is in our busy world, and attention spans are short.

In these sections, I get straight to the point of the chapter with no stories or extras - just what you need! More importantly, they take only a few minutes of your precious free time to read. So, if that's all you have available before bedtime, then at least some progress has been made on improving yourself as well as potentially preventing future problems down the line.

PART I - SEEDLING STAGES

The Seedling Growth Stage is the time when a family has grown to an extent that they are no longer just one person's dream. It might be hard work, but their dreams don't seem impossible anymore. Dads have more confidence in their ideas, identity, abilities and find themselves working in a much larger way, with many people contributing to the growth of their child.

As an investor dad you are willing to take on risks and put more energy in, because you carefully planned and prepared a foundation and surrounded yourself with a team of experts. You can see potential for big returns down the line if circumstances go well.

<u>Chapter 1 - The Infant and The Provider</u>

I thought being a dad was going to be easy. I had no idea that it would take more than 50 hours of caregiving in the first week alone! The challenges of parenting are much bigger and more complex than I ever could have anticipated.

The first few weeks after my daughter was born were the most demanding and difficult of my life. I had to learn how to take care of a baby while also trying to maintain some semblance of a work-life balance, which meant that during the day I was either at home with her or in the office working on projects. And it turned out that my wife also needed more of my love, time, and support as well. I had to stop what I was doing and go get her or come back home early from work if she fell asleep.

Before experiencing those first weeks of actual dad life, my plan was to make enough money so that we wouldn't have any worries. I thought if I made enough money, it would be easy to take care of and feed my child when she came into this world. And no one would have to worry about anything again, no matter how hard the times were, if I just had enough money to solve the problem.

I quickly realized that you can't buy your way out of the Infant stage. I wanted to get rich quick, so I thought buying a bunch of stuff like a bigger house, nice car, or whatever I wished for would make me happy.

I wasn't thinking about the joy of parenting, when it's just you and your child for hours on end or being able to watch her grow in real time with no filters. Just living moment-by-moment, watching as she tumbles her way into learning how stand up or says her first words. I wasn't measuring my life in those terms or with that metric in mind.

I didn't think about the 1 am feedings, then 3 am bed-wetting sessions, or 5 am jet lag for months on end. There was no ÜberEats, or laundry service, or even sleep deprivation medication I could order on demand. With a baby, you can't just hit snooze on your alarm clock and start the day over. You have to be committed to the job, to the work; it's yours to do.

My perspective changed from hunting and bringing home the kill, the bacon, the cheddar, the money, to being present for her, making sure she is happy and loved. I learned that parenting is about taking care of yourself so that you are able to take care of others.

I realized how wrong the money mindset of "Money is a resource, and I can store it, then used it to solve all of my problems," was. This idea is what I was focused on and the reason why I was obsessed with making more money. It was my tried, true, and tested model for years before becoming a parent.

Then, I learned a better description of money and how it is a magnifier, "Money simply amplifies its surroundings."

If you have money and you do good, your goodness and generosity are amplified, as are the financial returns. The opposite is true if you are bad and do cruel things. Money will also magnify those results in your life. The selfish become more selfish, and the greedy become greedier. This magnification explains why so many who win the lottery lose their earnings and go broke after a few years. They don't understand abundance or how to manage their money. So, they spend their prize or just try to make more by gambling on bigger scratch tickets, sport bets, or more risky speculation. They continue to look for the next big win. Or they live in a world of lack, not really understanding how money works. So, their money just amplifies their fears.

Because I was raised by struggling immigrant parents and watched them live pay-cheque to pay-cheque, my fear was that I didn't have enough. My parents always told me we couldn't afford it or don't have money for that. But if they had the chance, they came back and bought it when it went on sale. This habit is what made me hoard like my parents. I never used more than necessary and felt guilty about using too much while watching others with plenty get up from a meal without picking at their plate.

My journey as a father really showed me the cracks in my old money mindset and approach to living. And it made me think of what I was teaching my girls about money. What did they learn from the way I reacted or how I handled financial matters? I knew I wanted to set up my daughters with a more empowering mindset around money than I received. I wanted to pass on important lessons about money and how to use it, feel about it, my blueprint around its use, and the financial realty of our situation.

If you bought this book by chance, congratulations! You are among the top eight percent of wealthiest people on this planet. Many people around this world have no running water, electricity, or know where their next meal is coming from. Over half the earth's population lives on less than a dollar per day. So, I want to implant this thought in your head: compared to the rest of the world, you are already very wealthy. Start acting like it, and more importantly, be grateful for your wealth.

I am guilty of taking our simple luxuries for granted, like when I turn on the tap to wash my hands with perfectly fine drinking water. Kids in Africa have to travel two kilometers or more to pump a well for the same amount of water for the week. Or when I run to a public bathroom stall and realize there is no toilet paper, but I forget someone in South America has to squat behind a tree and wipe with leaves. Even when I'm hangry, rifling through the fridge and cupboards, past the cans and snack boxes looking for a tasty treat, there are families in Asia who decide which child gets to eat today and who has to wait until tomorrow to get their ration of rice.

Perspective is what we need. That reminder that most of us reading this book have it good. As parents, we may fight about money with our spouse or stress out about whether we have enough to feed our family or keep a roof over our head. But if we took a good look at our luxury items, a bed, running water, toothbrush and toothpaste, hopefully you realize you could live with a lot less. Appreciate your luxuries rather than looking for the next lottery ticket or increasing your human comforts. Instead look at the homeless in your neighbourhood or families in Third World or war-torn countries. Instead of watching a sitcom, maybe watch a documentary on how the rest of the world lives on a less than a dollar a day.

Focus on what is truly essential. Do we really need that extra pair of shoes or that dessert order or even that second vehicle for the weekend? I used to subscribe to the "You can have it all," mentality of success. But I found out being excellent in one area may mean that you fail in other fields. These sacrifices are called missed opportunities cost, but I refer to them as trimming the fat, or narrowing my focus. I used to pride myself being a jack of all trades. But something happened when I focused my energies and cut certain items out of my life. The other areas along the branch began to flourish because of this pruning or paring technique.

Starting a family with an infant is like starting an investment account. As fathers, we invest our money, time, and resources into raising children to make them successful adults. The analogy can also help us think about how much energy we should put into parenting as well as what type of parent each child needs in their life. That is where the first PAIR Method comes into effect. Every infant needs a provider.

I thought my role as a provider meant that I just need to bring home lots of money to address any issues, problems, and emergencies, so everything would be okay. But being the provider for an infant turns out to be so much more when you actually get to know them.

I had to take on a lot more responsibility than just earning money for my family and leading the household. As it turned out, I was also responsible for my infant's development. As a dad, your responsibility at this infant stage is to be a provider, educator, and protector. This point is when I had to learn a new word: Humbled. The responsibility of being the parent has humbled me for life.

This stage in parenting requires you to have an emotional connection with your infant that you'll need. A bond or pair.

Parenting is about providing them safety and trust and bestowing on them all the tools that will help their development at this early age so they can grow up happy and healthy. You are also responsible for teaching them how to connect with other people and basic social skills.

And yes, crying is a communication style. I was humbled to learn the number of things babies try to communicate to us, through their different cries. They try to let us know when they need help, want attention, they are uncomfortable because of a dirty diaper, or when they are completely exhausted, just like us dads.

This stage was the point I realized that parenting is a lifelong pursuit and if you don't invest in it, your kids won't be emotionally healthy. If they're not happy with themselves then there's little chance that they will be successful or wealthy when they grow up. We need to make sure our children are content people at this early stage. We can create stronger bonds between us which will help them become strong adults who have good emotional intelligence and feel confident about their abilities to succeed in life.

Being an investor also made me a better dad because investing gave me more money for my family while creating time for me to spend with my newborn baby. It helped me to balance out how much work I needed to do without having too many balls up in the air, like starting or running a business, marketing or administrative duties, and the many hats that entrepreneurs face today.

Self-awareness was the key to making my investing practice successful. No one needs a guru or advisor telling them what they should do with their money, but we all need help figuring out who we are in order to live a more fulfilling life. I found peace of mind from investing financially for so many years and understanding how it benefited me and my family.

With this awareness about myself as an investor, I made sure our kids saw firsthand the responsibility involved when situations get difficult: buying stocks at certain prices, trying new strategies even if they fail occasionally, and knowing that there will be ups and downs along the way. These fluctuations are why you need to keep your emotions stable throughout this process.

The most important point about this infant and provider pair is that dads and their egos may have to take a back seat because moms are the main providers at this infant stage. Dads, unless you magically grew a pair of life-giving sacs of milk on your chest, move over, and let the moms do what they were built for and have a natural gift for.

The body of your infant's mother undergoes some massive transformations. And those changes also extend to her hormones, her chemical balance, and even the way she thinks! She's hardwired to provide for this life outside of her body instead from inside it. If you can handle all that in a sleep deprived state with grace, then consider yourself lucky because you will witness an amazing transformation, right before your eyes.

The relationship between mother and infant is the most powerful. It can be hard for mothers to balance everything because they often feel the sole responsibility and pressure to provide for their newborn child. But a husband or partner should always carry some of that weight, so she doesn't have all the burden placed on her shoulders alone.

Be of service to your wife in other ways, like loving her unconditionally, encouraging her, and recognizing her efforts. That way, both you and she will be able to expand your love beyond each other, to experience not just a marriage, but a family. The mother of your child was able to birth you a gift of another relationship, one between father and child. That gift will bring you so much incredible vitality, joy, and purpose.

The mother of your child makes miracles happen. And you, dad, your job at this stage is to support the primary provider of the infant. Keep the perspective that she is running the marathon of motherhood. She will need fuel. She will need motivation, applause, and a cheer squad. She will need rest as she gives life from her body, a few hundred milliliters at a time. That effort requires a tremendous amount of energy because the mother is making, transforming, and providing for your child.

So, remember, dad, there is a lot of energy poured into this infant stage. And 90% of those needs are not dependent on money. Those necessities come from the primary provider, so your role switches to nurturing the mother who literally gives herself and everything she has to feed your living legacy.

The CEO Who Also Takes out the Trash

If you think that this section is about diapers, guess again.

As a new dad or soon-to-be father, your whole world will be shaken upside down. And your will, your energy, your patience, your love, your resolve, and especially your self-worth, will be tested like never before. Most new dads don't think about this but that's just because they're not thinking like an investor, they are just trying to survive.

So, here's the thing, if you want to thrive as a father and be really invested in your children, then you have to rethink what it means to provide for them. Fatherhood doesn't stop with providing food, shelter, or clothing. These are necessary, of course, but there are other things your child needs from their dad too, like emotional security, assurance of love no matter what happens, consistency (especially when life gets messy), protection against harmful influences outside the home, and support during difficult moments. These elements all take time and attention.

You may also have noticed that your marriage relationship and dynamic has changed a bit. You have less time for date nights and the random chats about nothing that you once had. That's because parenting now takes up a lot more of your day, and it consumes all of your attention.

Babies are especially needy little buggers, and they need us NOW, not later or tomorrow. They don't have patience to wait until we get around to them, which is probably why they cry so much! So, realize that you may be deprived of sleep, short on patience, and lowest on the family priority list for a while.

I got bumped off the winner podium in my marriage with my wife early on. It happened one day while parked outside of a grocery store, with a pregnant wife who didn't want to leave the car because she was tired. We always did everything together, and this incident was the first time she chose the baby instead of us. My wife was always a team player, always willing to be a part of the action. But in an instant, she opted out, the first small crack in our team.

I don't know why I took notice of her behavior that day, but the team dynamic shifted from a "just-the-two-of-us" honeymoon to a new hierarchy where our child took priority. It was a dynamic where I was no longer first place, not even second place in priority, but barely on the third spot of the podium.

For most guys, it is amazing to find that person you can tolerate or to finally get to the place where one person completes you and treats you better than you treat yourself. And we when finally get the courage to commit ourselves publicly to this one person, then we have to go through several mental shifts. We must work through the paradigms of lifelong commitment, self-acceptance, self-worth, and partnership. And in this new norm of dual income, no kids, we create a certain division of labour and shared responsibilities.

But with a baby on the way, my team member shifted focus. In the corporate world, this shift is considered a reallocation of resources, energy, and effort. Our dream partnership company had a shift in direction. The "board" restructured the "company," and I got bumped from my cushy executive position.

My lovely wife, through an acquisition, gained enough shareholder votes to oust me, and she became the dictator on how this newly structured company would run. Who knew that she would take the top spot, give up her employment status and income, yet endow me with all the janitorial and mailroom duties? This corporate restructuring is something I want to prepare you for, because it is an essential lesson to learn how to gracefully and gratefully go from King of the Castle to Her Majesty's Servant.

This phase as the provider during the pregnancy/ infancy stage requires you to become polite and kind in your behaviour, especially in a difficult situation. Being the provider is about your ability to move. Will you shuck and jive? Can you be the CEO and take out the trash? Is any task to minor for you to do?

The attitude shift that you will have to endure during this phase will come without warning. It may be a gradual shift or a sudden moment, but this shift into parenthood will become obvious. The most supportive evidence of this change will be found at the infant stage.

For me, that moment occurred in the car with my wife, when she did not go with me to find the items to build a gift basket for her sister-in-law. This moment was the first time my wife's acts of service were not exercised or, as we say in the investment world, not actively traded. She reallocated her funds; her energy was redirected into creating a miracle, my baby

I felt hurt by this huge void because I was not given the attention or acts of love I was accustomed to receiving from her in our relationship. My wife gave away what was once given to me, and now transferred that attention to our baby. Yet, this is my job: to show her love more than she could ever imagine possible. Investing in me makes this investment worthwhile.

The baby wasn't even born yet, but it was the first time I realized that my wife would have less time for me because of the baby-making effort and her own language of touch. Our initial ways of giving and receiving love made a dramatic shift. I had a really tough moment when I wanted my old life back. I wanted my wife and our old love dynamic.

So, when this moment occurs for you, remember if we dudes were to feel nauseous, kicked from inside, and deprived of rest and sleep for nine months, we might not carry ourselves as graciously as our counterparts. Think about the energy and how much it actually costs to make life.

I encourage you to think about the practical aspects of your partner's commitment and investment. Think about how much IVF, surrogacy, or adoption costs and ask yourself how much this choice has cost her.

And because of her intense effort and upfront "down payment," you now have a child to love and nurture. Imagine how much your partner has invested in this life that she created with you. She essentially birthed your first employee and gave you the gift of someone who will carry on your legacy.

So, I wish you luck with onboarding and orientation with your partnership, growing your business, and dealing with corporate restructuring. Remember, if this company is to survive corporate restructuring, the loss of income, and the shareholder majority ownership change, it is up to you, the CEO to rebalance your portfolio. For dads, this means looking at all areas of your family, from budgeting on a single income, to which rooms are designated for what purpose, to the household chores, duties, and responsibilities that need to be shifted or changed, temporarily or permanently.

As in all business start-ups and new young families, you'll have to factor in more investment cash or reallocation for this new venture. So, recognize that sweat equity will make or break your success when scaling your company, aka adding another family member.

3-PARE CHALLENGES

During the global pandemic, the government and society encouraged us to do only what was essential. Those necessities included food, shelter, and water. But what are the essentials for a family that is just starting out? We must first identify the basics. Not wants but needs.

From day one, humanity has faced many hardships. War-torn cities and concentration camps are just a few of the struggles our great-grandparents had to deal with, not to mention famine and drought! During the time when Covid-19 hit us hard, it was important that we remain safe by staying home or taking precautions against getting sick. Our burden was cut out of and controlled our desires to gather or travel, isolating us in the comfort of our homes.

We are a generation spoiled with riches, instant gratification, global communication, and every desire on demand. It is no wonder that as we face this global lesson, the pandemic focuses us on our true needs and brings us back to the foundation of what really matters. I am probably the guiltiest of this privileged order-on-demand life, as I was used to getting packages delivered in one day or travelling wherever I wanted to with one of our many vehicles.

As we begin this journey of Fatherhood through the lens of an investor's mind, let me remind you of what is truly important as you enter a time of extreme challenge and self-resilience during this pandemic. This new life and relationship of "The Infant and The Provider" is going to take a few actions, commitments, and investments for it stay alive, beyond just food, shelter, and milk. So, before we fully emerge from this global lockdown, let's make sure that our home is a place that provides for the needs of our children, not just physically, but emotional and spiritually as well.

My challenge to you is to **pare** down your expenses by conducting an experiment to experience living like the rest of the world.

The world's average salary is $18,000 per year, $1500 per month, $50 per day. Perhaps a more shocking statistic is that more than half the world's population lives on $720 per year, $60 per month, $2 per day.

How do they manage to survive on so little? How do 3.8 trillion people meet their daily needs? You are probably one of those lucky people who earns and raises a family with more than $50 per day.

Dads, we may think we need this tool for work or deserve that extra coffee to make it through the afternoon, but I promise you, there is room to pare down our expenses, save a little more, and maybe even allocate it to your nurturing your young one. If 3.8 trillion other people can have their daily needs met with just $2 per day, I urge you to put yourself in their shoes when you are feeling financially strapped or facing scarcity.

My challenge to you is to try this action for just one day, one week, or one month.

ACTION: Take all your money, bank cards, or credit cards, as well as your payment apps, and place them in one "Don't not touch" folder. Leave just two dollars cash in your wallet.

CHALLENGE #1 - Spending Habit Test

See if you can avoid spending that money for a day. At the end of the day, take note of your thoughts and whether that exercise was easy for you.

CHALLENGE #2 - Feeling Strapped for Cash

Put just $15 cash into your wallet for the week. That amount is all that you can use for discretionary spending for the week for gas, entertainment, or dining out. Get your groceries, fill up the vehicles with gas, and plan out the next week before hiding those cards or removing apps from your phone. Again, take note of your thoughts daily for one week.

CHALLENGE #3 - Month-Long Money Lessons

Put $60 cash into your wallet and only spend that amount in a month. Of course, before picking your start date, stock up, fuel up, and plan before hiding your cards. But in this challenge, I want you to also pick a subscription service, a monthly expense, or another luxury or indulgence and do without it for one month. Disrupt your services for just a single month to see if you can live without. Take notes of how you felt or succeeded.

Tip: The true magic of these challenges is not to see if you can survive a day, a week, or even a month with less. This practice determines what you will experience and find out about your habits, spending, and the difference between needs and wants.

It is one thing to understand the concept, but it is another thing to feel and experience it firsthand. This type of learning promotes deeper change, giving a new behaviour or habit a better chance of rooting itself.

Give from the Saucer, Not from Your Cup

With so much providing, paring, and focusing on other people, I don't want you to forget about filling yourself up. Make sure you remain strong, even while supporting everyone else. Removing excess wants from our lives gives us more energy, time, and focus to grow the things we want, like more time with our loved ones or peace of mind when it comes to household budgeting on a single income.

I was always someone who gave everything I had, an all-or-nothing person. Until one day, the stress of work caught up to me and I burnt out in a blaze of glory, like fireworks on Independence Day or New Year's Eve. This breakdown happened about once a year for me, until my workload got heavier as my success grew exponentially. Then, I started burning out twice yearly instead. I was led into project work with film or tech but eventually my burnouts occurred every three months. I had to start taking frequent vacations to stave off the anxiety.

I pursued the life of a do-gooder because I felt I had to in order to live my own life with some feeling of success or freedom. Helping others was all that I could think of to help me keep up with those around me. It was what society expected from someone like me, always caring rather than just caring for oneself. I checked off everything on this list, never missing an opportunity to care about other people's issues so long as they fit into my schedule and were within driving distance.

I seemed to have it all on the outside, but I was broken inside. Instead of spending my time with family and friends like they wanted me to do, I spent money on expensive hotels, vacations, dining out, and splurging for premier club access so that my family would never want or need anything. I happily disposed of my money as long as someone in my family was happy because of what I did or helped them with.

I thought I saved enough money to splurge, to afford, to cover the costs, but I didn't have enough true wealth or health to pay its real price. My effort made sure that my family and the people around me felt no stress, no hunger, and no lack, but it cost me my soul, my vibrance, my life. And that exchange wasn't helpful to anyone, nor was it true caring or giving.

I found the answer to resolve my burnout, a way to truly care and give, without costing me everything. It cost me one flight to San Diego, a stay at the Sheraton Marina for an all-day intensive weekend commitment with personal life-coach Lisa Nichols. I found another way of understanding and relating to wealth and abundance. She said, "Your job is to fill your own cup, so it overflows. Then you can serve others, joyfully, from your saucer."

This quote allowed me to understand the importance of self-care and how it can lead to success in life, true wealth, and abundance. It's a reminder that when you are happy, healthy, and fulfilled, then you will be better able to serve others around you.

You may not have considered this concept before, but there are two sides to every coin. Your own well-being affects other people as much as your actions affect you. If we want to make our world a better place for everyone else, we must first take care of ourselves.

How does taking time for yourself help or hurt your relationships? What steps do you need to take so that your cup overflows with joy?

3-PEAR CHALLENGES

The following challenge is designed to grow your habits of happiness and fill your cup with self-care, well-being, and positivity. Like the coin with two sides, these exercises may not look like they help your family; they may even seem selfish to you. But trust me, this practice will inspire you and fill you up so you can show up fuller, more energized, more compassionate, and more understanding, willing and joyfully ready to serve your family.

My PEAR challenge is meant to inspire growth, a habit of self-care and joy that will fill your cup.

CHALLENGE #1 - Your List of Activities

Write a list of 100 activities that bring you life: old, new, big, small, bucket list items - just write them all down. Consider one hundred things you can do, experience, and enjoy, things that will refresh you and give you joy. Post your list somewhere visible for you or even in a public place in your home. You might be surprised that your wife wants to join, support, or experience these activities with you.

CHALLENGE #2 - Let's Get Physical and Active

Pick just one physical activity and schedule it this week. For example, get your vegetables from a local farm, go for a swim, make a hair appointment, or book a spa day. Then scratch it off the list.

CHALLENGE #3 - Exercise the Mind

Pick or add a mental activity that you can turn into a daily habit or practice. Consider reading up on a hobby or interest, practicing mediation, or setting up a gratitude journal. Commit to that mental exercise for 30 days.

This exercise will provide the opportunity for you to do a lot, as well as give a lot of yourself. This action is the hard work of investing in yourself which allows you to front-load your efforts and pour your energy into personal assets.

I often think of my self-care development and growth as a tree. I have to cultivate it, nurture it, value it, and give it the space to grow.

3-PAIR TAKEAWAYS

The Infant

A cry is the baby's way of communicating their needs. What is frustrating is that we don't see this noise as talking. But if you listen carefully, you might learn to recognize the five baby crying sounds defined by parenting expert Priscilla Dunstan.

"Neh" - Feed me, I'm hungry

"Eh" - I feel something coming up, burp me

"Eairh" - Rub my belly, I gotta fart

"Heh" - I don't feel good, I'm not comfortable

"Owh" - I'm so tired, I can't sleep.

The Provider

The primary provider is actually the mother. A baby needs their mom, for that life-giving milk. The infant is the most bonded with her at first, like a security blanket. Being a mom to a newborn is literally draining. As a dad, I know you are tired too, but it is time to dig deep, into the unconditional love well.

Make sure that you are filled and loaded up as well. Be mentally and physically strong and fill your heart with joy. You will want to give, and your family is going to make withdrawals from you. Charge up emotionally, like playing a favorite song or reflecting on a memory of victory or bliss. Whatever you choose, make sure it fuels you.

The Infant and the Provider

This relationship is very one-sided early on. You give and give and give some more. And the baby, literally, gives you shit. As a young dad, it is hard to see immediate returns on your investment when it costs you financially, physically, and mentally.

Try loading up in an area that is mutually beneficial. After working all day, running errands, checking off all the household chores, and checking in with the baby's momma, be sure to spend time with your infant. How about you get some skin-to-skin bonding or bottle-feeding time with the baby.

I call this re-up time, "Stay Calm and Snuggle On." This time allows you to change gears or just park yourself somewhere to hold the baby. Others I know have renamed this time as, "Sorry honey, I can't. I have the baby." Either way, just sit back, relax, and enjoy being present with your baby.

Chapter 2 - The Toddler and The Teacher

I believe the children are our future,
teach them well and let them lead the way.
— Whitney Houston

A toddler's life has infinite potential in every direction that they choose to go. At this age, parents can teach their children valuable lessons about living life well and reaching their full potential, even if their careers or professions don't make them famous or rich.

Children at the toddler stage are sponges. They soak up everything that the world presents them with. And children learn 90% of their habits by the age of three. Do you ever wonder where they learn how to behave, act, or treat others?

Who do they spend the most time with? Is it you? Is it mom? Or is it the videos they watch on the iPad or TV? I've certainly called in the screen babysitter more than a few times. Heck, if you are like me, sometimes you just need a break from the survival mode and all it takes to raise a toddler

As a new parent who kept a newborn baby fed and alive for longer than two years, you deserve a medal. But toddlerhood is NO TIME to let off the gas or put yourself on cruise control and just coast. It is time to up your game and reflect on how you are playing it, because your future is watching. Your toddlers observe everything you do. Like a mirror, they see your actions and are as sure as hell going to MIMIC them. That is how toddlers learn, they copy your words and actions, exactly how you do it.

This imitation is why so many little kids love doing laundry and dishes. They love pretending to cook in a kitchen because we prep and cook meals several times a day. What you show your toddlers makes all the difference.

So, I challenge you as parents to imitate the best parents in the world by copying and mimicking the ones you admire the most. In my industry, many investors look up to Warren Buffett. Many a novice investor achieved tremendous results by copying the same investment stock choices as Buffett. But the truly successful wealth investors also mimic Warren's strategies, techniques, and mentality when it comes to his style of investing.

Buffett learned this style from his mentor Benjamin Graham, a university professor who is known as the "Father of Value Investing." Graham's teachings focused on investment philosophy and psychology, which helped him grow his investment returns nearly 20% consistently for more than 20 years.

His key teachings around value investing were based around a few concepts like fundamental analysis, margin of safety, activist investing, and developing a contrarian mindset. Essentially

Graham ignored the stock market price, and he looked at the company and got to know its business and how it operated. After understanding the business, only then could he determine what the value was and what was the best type of investment to contribute.

Does this company need a new printing press to mass produce newspapers instead of typing each one? Does it need more skilled labour or a larger workforce to put together these tailor-made suits? Or does this company need to look at sourcing new alterative fabrics to help with clothing sales and profit margins?

As an activist investor, he often gave more than just money, but also his time, effort, and resources to ensure the management and the company thrived. Benjamin Graham often used his influence to give insight and analysis and to offer solutions that ensured his investments were fruitful.

If we take this approach to investing from "The Father of Value Investing," and apply it to parenting, we should look at our toddler like a young company. We should also invest our money, time, and resources in the growth and development of their gifts.

What are the metrics for raising great children versus growing a successful company? Investing in a company is easy because your portfolio can be measured daily, monthly, quarterly, or yearly with a specific stock price figure. But the true metric of any investment for me is the Rate of Return. This measure is what is what we should copy with our parenting.

We have to ask what we want to teach our children. What is the measurement of return? My wife's return metric was simple. She didn't want to raise an a$$hole. With all my coaching experience, I chose to turn that measurement into a positive. We wanted our first child to bring light, hope, and goodness into the world. So, with that result as our goal, we named her Catalina which means white light and blessing.

Our second daughter, while in the belly, was constantly kicking and stretching. When we first heard her heartbeat on the ultrasound machine, the feedback was like a sitting next to a LOUDSPEAKER at an EDM dance party. This child's four heart chambers thumped two staccato beats and one downbeat, laying down a sick bass beat. Up beat, down beat. We knew this child would be a force. So, we named her Kaydence, like a cadence or rhythm in music. She teaches me about the different paces of life and the changes in modes to operate in.

All children have their nature prepackaged with gifts upon delivery. But it is our job as parents to nurture those gifts, to imprint and teach good habits that will foster their innate talents. It is important to avoid habits that teach toddlers to turn to ice cream at every challenge, to yell at each other, or to stonewall and avoid a conflict. They are watching you to see how you deal with difficult situations. They will copy your actions and make them their own.

In the moment of heated passion, challenge, or even despair, I ask you to look at yourself in the mirror for just ten seconds. See what your child might see in that moment. Is this a lesson you want to teach your kid? Our emotional ugliness is something that is hard to hide from our families, even if we show the world only what we want to project. But behind closed doors, our loved ones get to witness our true selves in our weakest, most broken moments. For young toddlers who learn how to react in every situation from us, we desperately need to show them how to navigate those moments of pain, confusion, and hurt.

The repetition of routines and habits is how toddlers learn. When they see an action over and over again, it becomes imprinted in their minds. What routines are you reinforcing with your children? The trick is to physically get down to their level and see what they see. Can they watch you prepare dinner or how you clean the dishes afterwards? What you do and how you do it is probably how your toddler will act when they grow up.

I know it is easier to put on an educational show, like *Baby Signing Time* or the *Knowledge Network* where your toddlers learn from great teachers. But if you only rely on others for instruction, you set your children up to look outside the precious concept called family. If you want infinite returns, you need to invest in your role with your children and step into their world as their teacher. The way you teach your children is one of the most critical roles at this age before they enter the formal education machine.

Get your returns by investing in your toddlers. Be the brokerage that they turn to for information, the guide who helps them make deals. Develop this role by spending undistracted time with your child. Practice giving them, five minutes at a time, your pure focus and concentration. This focus trains both you and your child to pay full attention.

On average, an adult's attention span is just over seven seconds. The best levels of focus and concentration last about 18 minutes at the maximum. We have a long way to go to regain our forgotten powers of deep concentration.

Interaction is key in the magic relationship between teacher and toddler. As the perfect students, toddlers are primed to take in information, train to any level without prejudice, and remain flexible and malleable. Young children are a resilient and robust portfolio with a tremendous capacity for acquisition.

Do not miss this window of time to teach a foundation of what you believe are acceptable returns on your investment. The Father of Value Investing, Benjamin Graham expected a 20% return per year. He passed that desire onto Warren Buffett, who passed it onto my mentor Phil Town, who passed it down onto me.

Along with setting your expectations as an activist investor, you also have the privilege of teaching them how to do it. So, I teach my girls values like politeness, kindness, teamwork, emotional resilience, and patience. I expect them to say, "Thank you," "Please" and grace before meals. I teach them breathing techniques to put themselves into a calmer state, and how to value others by greeting them and saying goodbye with a kiss, a hug, or a smile.

Consider your types of returns; what do you want to see more of? Is it a skill with intrinsic value such as, how to box, how to be flexible, or how to replicate musical masterpieces on the piano? Perhaps the return is learning to swim, using baby sign language, reading the alphabet, or even playing baseball.

Whatever skill or lesson you choose to teach, I implore you to look at the extrinsic value and returns of teaching them the merits of virtue and character, like honesty, manners, fairness, compassion, forgiveness, and kindness.

Your children are watching, so lead by example, teaching through the method of mimicry.

Parental Guidance: Disney or Marvel?

We are often told that the people we surround ourselves with have a significant effect on our lives. However, this maxim is more than just a saying; it's actually a scientific fact! This concept doesn't just apply to those around us, but also to historical figures and even fictional characters. We can learn something from everyone in our life if we take the time to notice.

During the pandemic, our physical circle of influence was limited, restricted, and even cut off to certain people. This limit to real, human connection was a reminder of how important it is for us to choose mindfully the influences that come to us on our screens and devices.

For toddlers in this sponge stage, how they see characters interact, struggle, and triumph on their devices is how they model or frame their lives in similar situations.

The way toddlers learn how to play and how to react to various circumstance is modeled by the characters they see. So which ones do you show them? What do those characters represent or portray? The simple way to decide what your children watch is to choose who you want to be their teachers and role models. Who do you want them to learn from or imitate?

Do you want your toddler to grow up like Captain Marvel or Ariel from Little Mermaid? Captain Marvel portrays a strong, independent role model. She is athletic and shows strength by taking risks. Ariel, however, is a rebellious, naive princess who gives into her own desires and is not transparent with her father.

Each role model and character that your toddler watches should be reviewed by you before you feed that subtle suggestion to your children. The characters from movies and videos plant the seeds of acceptable behaviour in your kids.

Because the case could be made that Captain Marvel resolves her problems with violence and Ariel fights for her own beliefs and dreams, it is essential to keep open lines of communication with your children. Neither role is perfect, so it's your job to highlight the influences you want your children to model. It takes work to program, craft, and vet these influences, but you are the Parental Guidance rating and filter for your little ones.

Pare down and cut out those characters that don't support good lessons or teach your children how to behave, especially since there are so many influences or role models available. Choose who you want them to mimic or analyze the characters together. Cut out the rest and explain why those characters are not quality role models. Sciences states that you and your children are the average of the seven people you hang around the most, including the characters you watch.

When I was younger, TV shows like *He-man* and *G.I. Joe* summarized the moral of the program or the important lesson at the end of every episode. They gave life lessons, like always telling the truth, or what do to if power lines fall. Those lessons stuck with me along with the saying that is ingrained in my head, "Now we know and knowing is half the battle... G.I. Joe." The shows I grew up with were endorsed by a National Child Safety Council and were written purposefully. They were crafted stories that taught how life really works and gave a clear moral at the end to reinforce the message.

But most TV programs and films are created for entertainment value, not to reinforce or promote moral values. Even as I continue my work in the entertainment industry, I urge parents to examine and filter what their kids watch. Be careful about what programs you encourage your young children to consume.

Disney princesses are a big hit and all the rage with my youngest daughter. Yet I am conscious of how those movies land with her and what messages they send. Do they give her the best view of life and how to approach it? Or do they subtly tell my girls that someone will come to rescue and save them or that life will always turn out happily in the end? These stories often set levels of fantasy expectations in our children's minds.

The best way to prevent such fantasies is to be your child's role model. Show them how to handle life's challenges, how to celebrate wins, or how to be vulnerable and honest. Be an example of what to do in real-life situations and reinforce the message you want. Create the results or returns you want to see.

We all have heroes in our lives. They are the people we trust and admire for their strength, courage, and wisdom. As parents, it's important to instill these qualities in children at a young age so they can grow up with a strong foundation of what it means to be a hero and a confident person.

3-PARE CHALLENGES

Who is your role model? Is it someone who learns from their mistakes? Is it someone who is resilient and will always get back up again? Or is it a person who defied the odds and adversity to succeed? If you don't have a role model or if you don't choose one consciously to help or guide you, your unconscious will choose one.

One of the role models I chose for my daughters is Carol Danvers. She is an American female superhero from Disney and Marvel studios movie who becomes "Captain Marvel." I like to show my girls one specific scene, a flashback montage when Captain Marvel is knocked down repeatedly, as a superhero, as a fighter pilot, a new military recruit, a young girl, and as a daughter. At first glance, it seems like the greatest reel of EPIC fails and flops, but as the montage unfolds, the focus portrays the conviction on the character's face as she learns from each fall how to simply stand and get back up. This lesson is one that film portraits so elegantly. Just get back up.

In real life, getting back up after a fall is never as EPIC or glamorous as they portray it in the movies. Rarely do we ever get to see what resilience looks like. I encourage you to share that clip with your kids and show them what it looks like for everyday heroes to FAIL, bite it, lose it, but then stand back up.

You may not realize how much your life is impacted by the people you choose to watch on the screen. You might not even know the characters in the shows that your young toddler watches. Do you notice the film's rating icon at the beginning of those shows?

CHALLENGE #1 - Rate Your Children's Shows

Make a list of your toddler's favorite shows and research what the overall messages are, or if there is a lesson to learn from each episode. You need to act like the National Child Safety Council and give your endorsement or PG. You need to figure out if this show is something you want your toddler to emulate or copy. Your focus is to eliminate as many shows as you can, so your toddler can learn the important life lessons from you.

CHALLENGE #2 - Cartoons to Real-Life Examples

Introduce an educational show or real-life hero and cut out one fictional character for the month. In our house, *Paw Patrol* was a big hit. The five cartoon dogs represented a police officer, construction worker, recycling depot worker, fire fighter, and a search-and-rescue officer. Start introducing to your toddlers what the characters look like in real life. If you prefer animals or nature shows to show your toddlers, go see if you can track these animals in their natural habitats or visit them at a zoo.

CHALLENGE #3 - Meet an Everyday Hero

Cut out all fictional characters and movies from your children's influence. They need to relate to real people and real life, not be grounded in fantasy. You can introduce those influences when they get older. Go meet a real-life hero, such as a fireman, your local nurse, or an art teacher, someone who you admire or would like your child to grow into.

Copy-Cat Investing, Finding Cadence

It's a well-known proverb that, "The apple does not fall far from the tree." Parenting is an art and craft, with skills to be learned and augmented over time.

The apple doesn't fall far from the tree in this case because toddlers learn by example. Parents are their children's own best teachers. Children who see love, respect, compassion, generosity, and kindness at home will reflect these qualities as they grow up. Parents not only raise their own children, but they also raise the parents of the next generation.

It is so important to be mindful of the behaviors you portray in front of your kids. However, what many people don't realize is that there are some qualities we teach our children without even realizing it! Parents can even pass on their beliefs about money and wealth to their children through their everyday actions.

When a toddler learns a new notion, they are likely to copy it. From mimicking their parents' actions, facial expressions, and mannerisms, to repeating the words they say. My first child Catalina spent a lot of time with my mom. It is amazing to see how much she looks like my mom - her physical build, her facial mannerisms - these traits are expected. No DNA tests are needed to determine that she is from my lineage. But surprisingly, the habits and tendencies that reflect my mom are not genetically coded. The way Catalina talks and reasons, the way she hums when she works or focuses intently, or even the energy and confident vibes that she carries are imprints from my mom, her grandmother.

She is a direct and perfect Copy-Cat of me and the strong line that I belong to. A great first child to break us into the world of parenting. An easy traveller who slept anywhere, a good eater with a happy, social, and very attentive personality. She even took direction well and loved to learn and receive feedback. She was obedient, compliant, and very self-aware, the perfect first-born child. She helped us show all our friends what a breeze parenting was and how lovely kids were.

My wife and I joke that she was the reason why so many of our friends hopped on the baby bandwagon after interacting and seeing how easy raising a baby could be.

Granted, she was the first grandchild on both sides and the whole village, including our parents, our brothers and sisters, the extended grand-uncles and grand-aunts, and all of our friends surrounded her to pour love, attention, and helping hands to raise a wonderful daughter. A perfect Copy-Cat and representation of our amazing village.

My second daughter Kaydence was born a couple of years later. She was *not* like her sister. In the womb she already beat to her own drum. When she came out, she didn't want to eat, wouldn't latch or bond, and didn't sleep well. She did not like being outside her familiar environment and comfort zone. Her personality was most evident when she was a baby.

I thought I could raise her the same way I treated Catalina. I expected to be able to strap her to my chest in an Ergo baby carrier and go on with my business, just dragging her along. A happy-go-lucky baby.

My plan was a quick lunch date at a local café with my cousin from New York. Then, we would take a nice, relaxing stroll and chat through the shops of West Boulevard. What a wonderful and delightful afternoon I planned for us to catch up as I introduced her new niece, Kaydence.

Like all my wonderful plans, this one all went to shit. Kaydence didn't want to be strapped to my chest or to sit in her stroller. She wanted to be handled during lunch, and when that wasn't enough, she wanted to dominate the conversation. Her cries were loud enough that the other tables began to stare, implying that their acoustic environment was being assaulted by my unhappy baby.

Lunch plans were altered. I connected with my cousin outside through the front window of café while she finished her lunch quickly. I hoped we could move onto phase two of the plan, walking and talking while we shopped.

After a quick reset, a battle-royal diaper change, and a warm bottle, we tried a new tactic with an unfed daddy. I don't know if it was too windy, too cold, too hot, or the stars were misaligned, but Kaydence didn't want to sleep, rest, or sit during our walk. It was more like squirm, fight, and wail! Finally, we abandoned all my brilliant plans and backup ideas. I had to wave the white flag and surrender. We retreated home.

The moment we arrived, I put the car seat down on the living room floor and unbuckled Kaydence. She headed straight to her play table and her toys. I took the moment to grab my cold, leftover lunch. As I stuffed my face, my cousin said to me, "Wow, this is the first time I've seen Kaydence smile all day."

That moment, the first seedling sprouted, and I noticed that Kaydence might be a home body. She had a very different vibe from how our family typically operated.

What that afternoon taught me was that I can't just teach or force my wishes upon my children. Nor can I duplicate all my traits in them. I was lucky with my first but still, I had much to learn as a parent. And that realization is the gift Kaydence gave me. I learned not to rest on my laurels and my good habits but to grow and stretch my understanding as well as my flexibility.

Children are born with their own internal rhythmical beat and harmonic cadence. And as parents we should not expect our children to follow ours or copy-cat their siblings, because life is about exploring new rhythms and beats.

3-PEAR CHALLENGES

As your toddler follows you around, try to engage in some activities where they can observe you. Do some routine chores or a brand-new task, like building a piece of Ikea furniture. The challenges are designed to demonstrate to your toddler how you respond at different stages of the learning curve.

CHALLENGE #1 - Tour of the Chores

Include your toddler as you complete your chores. Focus on ones such as collecting and taking out the trash or washing the dishes or car while listening to music. Remember the toddler's only job is to watch you perform the task. If they see you enjoying your tasks, there is a better chance they will want to copy you.

CHALLENGE #2 - A Puzzle to Conquer

Grab a 500-piece puzzle and show your little one how to start, approach, and complete it. Kids need to see how you approach new projects, so show them the learning curve, how you problem-solve, and your excitement when you accomplish a prolonged task.

CHALLENGE #3 - Count your Progress Aloud

Your challenge is to find five minutes at the same time each day and do as many sit-ups/ push-ups as possible in that time. And for the next month, track your progress on your calendar. While you do your reps, have your toddler count with you. 1…2…3…4…

These challenges allow you to attain results in several different areas. You can accomplish your chores, teach your toddler how to do a task, and get mentally and physically fit in the process. And remember, everything is better when you jam to your favorite musical play list.

3-PAIR TAKEAWAYS

The Toddler

Toddlers are copy-cat machines. Be mindful of what you show them because they will mirror your habits and behaviours.

Some toddlers come pre-loaded with their own personalities, traits, and rhythms that differ from our own. Accommodating and embracing those differences can help up grow in patience, understanding, and empathy.

The Teacher

We are our children's very first teacher. As most of us don't have teaching degrees, nor are we formally trained as educators, here are some important elements to consider when assuming this role:

- Show your children, versus tell them. Demonstrate the task first.
- Appeal to all five of their senses, touch, taste, smell, sound, and sight.
- Add the element of fun and enjoyment. Playing is a great way to learn.

The Toddler and the Teacher

This pair is one of my favorite life stages. The bond that is created between toddler and teacher is one that you can lean on well into the seedling and growth phases of life.

It is the dynamic that is a solid foundation which other activities and hobbies are built on. A family that plays together, stays together.

While learning together, remember to encourage each other's efforts, acknowledge the progress, and celebrate the achievements and wins. You are building up memories and stacking on self-confidence as your child's attitude towards learning and development is formed. Always learning, always growing.

Chapter 3 - The Child and The Coach

At first glance, this chapter might seem the same as the last one, "The Toddler and The Teacher," but there is a significant difference between being a coach and a teacher.

My simplified distinction is whenever there is a need to acquire a new skill or knowledge, you'll need a teacher to educate you on the "what you need to know," the fundamentals. Teachers are trained to help expand the mind. A coach, however, helps you practice and develop those skills, advancing your abilities and increasing your competency. Coaches help others to find their zone.

It's hard to be the best parent you can be when you're also juggling a career, health, your own personal life, and being the expert on all subject matters. Parents often struggle to find the right balance between these areas, especially when determining these two roles of being a teacher or a coach.

Often, we sign up our children to attend the most convenient and economical place for classes, such as our closest community centre. Yes, it is easy to out-source production and learning to the many institutions that teach your kids better than you can. They often have more experience, patience, and more physical resources and tricks to train your children.

You may pay for someone to impart the skills, but the teacher is not paid to provide the drive, the motivation, or the care to succeed. They often aren't invested in your individual child. They simply want your money; they are a business after all. It is rare to find teachers who are coaches as well. I encourage you to lean into those people who have a vested interest in your children's development.

It is up to the coach to reinforce, support, practice, and retain skills. And that coach is you, Dad. Call this role the Dad Coach, Head Coach at home, or Team Family Coach. The more encouraging coaches you can surround your child with, the better. They will help them strive and reach their potential, interests, and goals.

All successful games, competitions, and even wars, entail a strategy to win or to gain victory. It is up to the coach to bring that strategy and develop, not only the skills and abilities of the players, athletes, and soldiers, but to build the belief that they can achieve it.

And that reason is why a coach is needed. To be a visionary to guide the team to win the championship. He sees the potential of the individuals and holds the space towards success. Whether the goal is to win one game, compete at the national level, or to take the stage for the first time, these accomplishments usually require a coach with the foresight to encourage the child to step up in the face of adversity, fear, and doubt. Coaches see beyond what any child can see. They envision a possible future and help guide the child in that direction, usually stumbling forward.

And as the Head Coach of your family, remember, there is no "I" in team. You will need an assistant coach, a practice coach, a mindset coach. Focus on how your family franchise or company is structured. Gather some founding members, like vested grandparents, on board. And work to build a supportive Coaching team.

Do You Have an A.N.T. Problem?

The world is a much more difficult place to navigate when you don't feel like you have the power to make decisions and control your life. That feeling is no different for kids.

As parents, we often say statements to our children that may not be in their best interests. We want them to have successful lives and make good choices for themselves, but sometimes we slip up and create messages that are disempowering.

I am a first-generation born Canadian. That reality means I am sandwiched, reconciling the differences between two separate worlds and their ways. My parents were raised in the Eastern world by parents who survived the era of the Great Depression and two World Wars. Because of that trauma, their parents' mentality and experience was one of lack, hardship, and struggle. This mindset may be why my parents' generation fled Asia, in search of a land filled with dreams, hope, and opportunities.

This generational experience reinforced certain cultural and societal habits adopted by many Asian children. One cultural norm was using corporal punishment, a parental dictatorship, and rule by the stick. Just showing the feather duster or slipper was enough to keep order in the home. Children were also fed a verbal diet of, "You'll never be able to do it." "I can't afford it." "You are too young to understand." And "Don't worry, you'll be fine when you are older."

Words and actions like these are designed to keep children in their place at the bottom of the decision-making process. They restrict children from growing, and they suppress their beliefs. These statements are demoralizing and critical, designed to put people down. Such actions don't instill openness, vulnerability, or even acknowledgement to children.

All of us, both immigrants and native-born people, have a voice inside our heads that usually tells us what we can or cannot do. It is that voice that tells you to give up when circumstances get tough, or the one that says, "I can't," or "I don't know how."

That voice is your Automatic Negative Thought (ANT).

The ANT will tell you not to start a project because it might be too difficult. It discourages you from applying for the job of your dreams because the company won't hire someone like you. It says not to go after what you want in life because your dreams aren't possible. The ANT inside our minds developed from years of listening to messages about who we are, where we come from, and what we're capable of.

It is our job as Coaches to first identify what our own limiting statements, thoughts, or beliefs are. The next step is to recognize where those ideas came from. Remember when and where that negativity was first planted in your head.

It is only when we understand what negative belief we are dealing with, how long it's been there, and how deep it is rooted in our life, that can we start to break it. No matter how old you are, no matter what your circumstances, you can change the way that story is being told in your life and what you tell yourself.

3-PARE CHALLENGES

The old saying, "Sticks and stones may break my bones, but words will never hurt me," just isn't true. Words are powerful. They can build us up or tear us down.

Do you ever have those days when you wake up and it feels like the world is against you? You start to remember all the bad situations that happened the previous week and your mood becomes bleak. This the self-fulfilling prophecy of negativity, and it is driven by your Automatic Negative Thoughts. Your ANT tells you how everything will go wrong today.

"I'll never get it right." "I'm not good enough." "That always happens to me." We need to limit ourselves from speaking these negative thoughts into existence in our external world. Even though this voice sounds comforting or familiar, the statements do not have your best interests at heart. Your brain is trying to keep you safe. That internal voice wants to keep you small, so you don't grow past your comfort zone.

This constant state of fear and unbelief is a toxic way to live. When we are disconnected from our own strengths, we give away our personal power to the external world. Most of the Automatic Negative Thoughts were not our ideas in the first place. They were usually planted in our minds by other people's beliefs and experiences.

The following challenges are designed to identify your own thoughts and desires. Take a look at what is there and examine if it serves and helps you, or if it hurts you. As a coach, you need to know what thoughts and beliefs have limited your own potential first before you can recognize and encourage growth in your child.

CHALLENGE #1 - Trap the Negatives

Take note of those pesty little automatic negative thoughts running around in your conscious and unconscious mind. Write down what you hear, the statements and exact words you hear. I want you to see them all in writing, to take inventory. It is necessary to understand what pests are taking up real estate in your mind.

CHALLENGE #2 - Dig and Expose the Roots

Dig a little deeper and identify the source of that thought or belief. Ask yourself these questions to help find the origin of your Automatic Negative Thoughts:

- When did I first get that idea?
- Who was the first person who said that to me?
- Is that belief something that I want to guide my life consciously or subconsciously?

CHALLENGE #3 - Farewell Ceremony

Use a clearing exercise to bid farewell and goodbye to limiting beliefs and other negative statements that may or may not be your own. Mourn them, write them down, then remove these limiting and non-serving statements by burning them, turning them into ash. I always recommend that you do this final step outdoors and in a safe manner.

These challenges will hopefully help you identify some of those negative thoughts and statements that you say to yourself. I encourage any dad or parent who has a hard time letting go of these thoughts to reach out to a trusted, honest friend or professional to help you uncover and reveal some of these subconscious beliefs that hold you back.

Recruiting your Board of Directors

There is no such thing as a self-made man. We are made up of thousands of others. — George Matthew Adams.

In order to be successful and fulfilled, we need to have the right people around us. As a head coach for our children, it is important to gather the village that includes our family, friends, mentors, and financial professionals who are committed to guiding us through life's transitions and opportunities with honesty.

In the investment and business world, our head coaches are called CEOs (Chief Executive Officers), and the teams they help manage and run are their companies. Because I take the business of family very seriously, I wanted to pull from areas that I see great coaches really focus on. These elements include belief, mindset, and problem solving, not just sport, recreation, and entertainment.

Even if you have never owned a business or started your own company, the general breakdown of typical corporate structure can provide a beneficial model in your family. Big Fortune 500 companies, or publicly listed companies usually have a successful system in place to guide and manage thousands of people and millions of dollars. Why not use that same leadership model and apply it to the family structure?

One of the secret weapons of large companies is their executive or leadership team, typically called a Board of Directors. In the sport coaching world, the board would include your assistant coaches and scouts. Typically, a Board of Directors is comprised of vested and experienced individuals who help guide the company.

Many powerful and influential people sit on boards to help grow their companies. And usually they are invested, holding shares or a part-ownership of the company. Their interests are tied to the performance of the company. They are financially rewarded when the shares they hold increase in value.

These directors can be divided into two groups. Inside directors are usually shareholders or high-level managers from within the company. Outside directors have the same duties but are not part of the management team. Their purpose is to provide an unbiased and outside perspective. They are usually industry experts and respected leaders in their own fields.

The directors are led by a chairman or a chairwoman who is responsible for running the board smoothly and effectively. Together, they are responsible for monitoring the company's management team and advocating for the investors and owners, typically known as shareholders or stockholders.

So how does this business model fit into a family structure or in the business of family? My family's "board of directors" includes both sets of grandparents. They are inside directors since they are investors and part owners. My brothers and sisters are also inside directors. One easy distinction for me is if there is a blood relationship, they are listed as an inside director. They are usually closest to the company (family), and they directly or indirectly impact your child's development by reinforcing your family's beliefs.

Then, there are outside directors, such as family friends, godparents, other successful parents, investors, and role models who have a vested interest in your children and their future. They are great advisors on how to manage parenthood or have mutual interests because their children go to the same school.

All of my children's teachers, instructors, and caregivers, are considered the management board or coaching staff of our family's company. They are in charge of the day-to-day operations. The schoolteachers help with academics like reading and writing. The swim instructors help with practicing life skills. And the caregivers encourage healthy social habits with their peers.

Remember, you are the Head Coach, and while your focus is on developing your child abilities and belief mindset, you don't have to do it alone, nor should you. Work with teachers and build upon their lessons, like two hands synchronized together, the left and the right.

I want to take you a step further, from being a coach to thinking like a CEO. If you can think of your family as a business, you'll want to recruit the best advisors, specialists, and board members to help grow your company, your children. The good news is that these people might be in your family already. You won't have to pay a board of director's salary for them to mentor their grandchild, niece, or nephew. Maybe they'll take payment in-kind instead, like a nice family dinner. A family that eats together, stays together

3-PEAR CHALLENGES

The power of the team you surround yourself with will determine how successful you are in life. This lesson was taught to me by one of my favorite coaches Phil Jackson, a basketball coach who won 11 championship rings over 20 seasons, with more than one team. He is most famously known for coaching some of the best players in his field, taking them to unbelievable success, on and off the court. Michael Jordan, Shaquille O'Neal, and the late Kobe Bryant are a few of the greats under his tutelage.

But Jackson didn't do it alone. While operating as the head coach of the Chicago Bulls, he was hired, recruited, and supported by CEO and owner Jerry Reinsdorf. Reinsdorf was a successful investor, so much so that he owned two professional sports in Chicago, the Bulls and the White Sox. He sat on many boards as a director for other successful companies like Lehman Brothers, LaSalle Bank, and Northwestern University.

You have to think, not just of your child's development, but about how to grow that management team around your child. Start with blood relatives, especially their grandparents, uncles, and aunties. These are the people who will love on them and pour experience and knowledge upon them that you cannot teach all by yourself. I hate to break it to you, but you can't know or be the best at everything.

Are there any other role models or people you want your child to grow up to be like? Are there skills, habits, or mindsets from people outside your family that you wish your children to know and learn from?

The following challenges are designed to help you get back into the game and to become familiar with the coaching landscape.

Remember, the outcome isn't just to learn a new skill, but to learn the process, and how great coaches lead their teams. So, as you go through these challenges, remember to take note of how you were coached, encouraged, recognized, and pushed to grow.

CHALLENGE #1 - Trains the Trainer

Find yourself an art class or a sport team you can attend with at least four sessions. Attend one session every week for a month. Discover what it is like to be a student again, to have someone else teach you a skill, coach your development, and take notes so you can turn around and do the same for your child. Find out how you like to be coached.

CHALLENGE #2 - Can You Teach My Child?

Ask a relative or a close friend that you admire to teach your child something new. It can be as simple as folding paper airplanes to something more complex like how to bake a cake. Watch and take notes on how your child learns, processes information, and where your child is uncomfortable or needs a gentle nudge or words of encouragement. Watch how your child responds to coaching.

CHALLENGE #3 - Becoming Students Together

Enroll in a Parent and Child class, where you will both do an activity or learn something new together. Pick something that interests your child but challenges you both. Perhaps try out a dance class or a bike maintenance course.

Be humbled by how quickly children can learn, and let's give them the opportunity to be the expert. As you do the challenges, watch how they develop an attitude of learning and encouragement that reflects your own.

3-PAIR TAKEAWAYS

The Child

We all know that children are sponges and will pick up on everything we say. It is important to make sure your messages are positive!

It's been shown that when children have a coach in their lives, whether for academics or sports, they have better grades and higher test scores. When our children are coached, they have another voice or external motivator who encourages them to push on. Yes, it is hard, but it is possible, and they can do it. This encouragement from coaches leads to children who have increased self-esteem, creativity, and critical thinking skills.

The Coach

Being a coach brings another layer to our teaching. As teachers, we give knowledge or introduce new skills. As a coach, we take the lessons one step further and nurture our children's abilities, mindsets, and beliefs.

We need to give them our belief, as show them the potential that we see in them. And for some of us, it has been a long time since we have been coached ourselves. My recommendation is that you put yourself in your child's shoes, where the learning curve is steep, and take note how you need to be supported, motivated, and encouraged to press on.

In order for us to coach well, we need to know how we like to be coached ourselves.

The Child and The Coach

The coach is needed at all life stages. Professional basketball players need them to win championships. Grade Three math students need them to make sense of new techniques. The coach is a positive voice that is seeded into our inner child, so that when we feel discouraged, fearful, or unsure we can recognize that inner encouragement. We might hear that coach's voice acknowledging, "Yes, the task at hand is difficult, but you are capable of doing it. Keep going and take it easy. You'll get it."

The more caring and mindful coaches you surround yourself and your children with, the more of a chance that when you fall, you'll be cushioned by a coach to pick you up, mentally and physically.

Chapter 4 - The Pre-Teen and The First Responder

Every parent knows that their children are growing up and becoming more independent mentally and physically. But have you ever thought about how your child is maturing emotionally?

This chapter will explore the question of how to manage the emotions of a pre-teen. As a parent, it is important to understand what qualities make up a pre-teen's emotional state, as well as some strategies for navigating these ever-changing feelings.

No two pre-teens are the same. Some may be more mature than others. Some may have experienced a difficult life event that made them insecure and sensitive to criticism or bullying from other children. Still others might just need to find their way through this new stage of development.

Regardless of what your child is going through right now, it's important not to overreact when they're upset about their circumstances. All too often, we can't see past our own feelings as parents to understand how our pre-teens feel about themselves.

Our pre-teens really just need us to show up when there is an issue that they are dealing with. And I can't think of a better group of real-life heroes whose job it is to literally show up and assist where they can than First Responders. You may think of fire fighters, paramedics, or emergency medical technicians; first responders are those who arrive and assume authority to administrate the appropriate care.

Now, I am not saying to treat all your pre-teens' interactions like they are an emergency situation, but I am encouraging you to carry yourself like a first responder. How do first responders show up to a scene after they received a call? Do they run frantically to the front door, ready to do chest compressions? No, they calmly walk with their bags and equipment prepped in hand, attentive and alert.

This calm and efficient manner is the same demeanour and approach I want you to take with your pre-teen. You can't just leap into parenting your pre-teen without doing the work upfront.

Think about those moments when a pre-teen is feeling overwhelmed, and everything goes haywire. They might start screaming or crying or yelling at their mother for no reason. Maybe they are upset because someone wasn't giving them enough attention, even if that person was themselves. That is where being calm comes in handy. It's not always easy, but your demeanor will help keep the situation from escalating too quickly.

Your pre-teens need to associate you with being their personal first responders. When they feel insecure, unsafe, or overwhelmed, they need to have the confidence to call upon your help and services. Simply answering their call is enough; being there for them is a win. And in most cases, your presence is all they need, a sympathetic ear, the reassurance that they matter as they go through an emotional situation or challenging incident.

Parenting is about being there for your pre-teen son or daughter as they grow up and need you the most. It's time to show them that investing in their life means more than just money.

I would have benefited from such investment when I was a pre-teen. Yet, there was no one to call and talk to about how I felt when I was rejected. All of those emotions were bottled up inside me for way too long. As an adult, these experiences seem so tiny in perspective, but they had such a deep impact on my psyche at the time. In retrospect, I wish my dad had come home early from work and entered the front door like a first responder with a bag of emotional tips and tricks to fix my broken heart.

Any proper emergency response kit should include a patient assessment checklist for the first responder to refer to:

- Date and time of injury
- First reported to
- Chief complaint
- Vitals signs
- Injured/ exposed areas
- Physical findings
- Interventions/ treatments
- Recommendations
- Follow up

But more important is how the first responder conducts the assessment and how that method makes the patient feel. Dads, note that people in distress seem to calm down or experience relief when they see a first responder on the scene. The reputation of first responders is one of aid, support, and help. Their training and skills put patients and bystanders at ease by gathering all the facts, asking really good questions, and taking notes in a calm, experienced manner.

You'll notice over 85% of the first responder's checklist is for gathering information. For dads, that translates into listening more for the purpose to understand than to fix the situation. So, think of yourself as a first responder and ask leading questions that aid in gathering information and understanding your pre-teen's story.

The first time a pre-teen experiences heartbreak, it can be difficult for parents to know how to help. Pre-teens are still learning how to manage their emotions and the complexities of life in general. It's important that we don't try and make the situation worse by blaming or shaming them. We should instead work with them through this difficult time. Be present and allow them the time and space to heal after being hurt. Self-care is vital for emotional health.

Fairy Tales vs. Real-Life Stories

As parents, we do our best to shield our children from life's realities. We tell them they can be anything and everything they want to be. But how do you deal with the day-to-day reality of managing a pre-teen who is becoming more aware that their dream career or their first relationship may not pan out? A good place to start is by understanding that it's never too early to have conversations about realistic expectations with your kids.

Do you remember the story of Cinderella? The girl who was mistreated by her stepmother, stepsisters, and fate but nevertheless found love in the end with a prince. It's an inspiring tale that has been retold throughout generations to teach girls about what it means to be strong and persevere.

But not all princess stories end well. Take Princess Diana who did not find her happily ever after. Or how the modern-day version of a princess Meghan Markle discovered that she romanticized the idea of a royal life, but was not fully aware of the realities, tension, and real-life stress it would cause.

Recent research shows that children who are exposed to more reality-based stories tend to have a higher self-esteem than those who read fairy tales. Fairy tales are great sources of inspiration, and I love a great story, but some tales are just that - fantasy and not REAL life. It is important for parents to teach their children honest expectations of what is real life and what is just a fairy tale or fantasy.

We must cut out the expectation that we will never get hurt, especially for those of us who are dreamers. We are going to get hurt when we push beyond our comfort zones. That discomfort is how we grow. We must endure the pain, the suffering, and the heartbreak. That understanding is why it is so important at this stage in our children's lives to cut out certain influences or ungrounded and unrealistic expectations. Achievement and growth are essential to a child's development but note that the road is not without pain. Any road worth travelling has to cost something.

As parents, our job is to provide a true and realistic understanding of what love is, and the difference between fairy tale love and real-world love.

It's important for parents to allow their pre-teens to make mistakes. In order to learn and grow, they need to experience the consequences of their actions. As a parent, you can help guide them through this process by coaching them on how to deal with various situations so that they don't go down the wrong path. Or, if they do choose the wrong path, they know how to make a U-turn or how to find their way back home.

Many parents don't want to let their pre-teens fail. They want to protect them from the pain of disappointment and mistakes, but in doing so, they rob their children of a chance to learn how to be resilient. We must be ready and on standby to answer the call for help when we see them face a difficult decision. Consider creating a text code or secret emoji signal your child can use when they need help.

We need our kids to take risks and make mistakes so that they can grow into successful adults who are able to thrive in an unpredictable world. They will have to learn how to deal with rejection and disappointment in their lives, so it is best to learn those lessons under your roof and guidance.

3-PARE CHALLENGES

We have all been there. The day our child starts to become a pre-teen is the scariest day of our lives. And when that first argument ensues, we are ready to give up and resign from parenting altogether! It can be hard to not feel hurt or disappointed when they make decisions that go against what we would choose for them.

Parents want to make sure their children are ready for what's coming later in life: college, career, marriage. But before we think about these more distant future events, it's important to teach them how to handle the here and now.

One practice, that helped me cut through all the distractions and emotional chatter was to focus on breath work. Breathing is a practice that every person can do. Your breath is an action that is constant, and one that your pre-teen can literally count on.

When your preteen feels overwhelmed, in their heads, or spiraling down, they may get lost in their emotions of disappointment, jealously, insecurity, and fear. Teach them to cut out all the stresses and bring themselves back to their body, into the present, by breathing in deep.

Have your children fill their lungs, holding their breath for three seconds, then count as they breathe out. This simple technique calms the mind and allows pre-teens to weather their emotions, not control them. Breath work gives them a way to anchor the mind and body in the midst of the emotional rollercoaster and storm.

The following challenges are designed to identify and eliminate stories and unrealistic expectations in real life. These stories might be fairy tales from childhood, but in today's world those fantasies might be social-media influencers. Often these influencers don't portray their full experiences but only show a curated version of their best life.

CHALLENGE #1 - Flush out Negatives

Cut out fairy tales or unrealistic influences of love or relationships. That also means cutting out social media influencers or people who portray unhealthy or unsustainable lifestyles. Cut these narratives out of your pre-teen's screen and do the same for yourself as well.

CHALLENGE #2 - Name and Color your Feelings

Look up Putchik's Emotional wheel. Print it out and post it on the fridge or another conspicuous place. The image looks more like a dart board, with many rings expanding out from the centre. Each segment is filled with a different emotion and a different color. The emotions and colors are more intense near the bullseye. Color in each emotion with Putchik's corresponding color profile for that emotion whenever you or your pre-teen experience it.

CHALLENGE #3 - A Personal Hand-Written Letter

In a letter addressed to your pre-teen, write about a time when you felt emotional, hurt, or broken. Conclude with how you overcame your struggle, healed from it, and what that resilience taught you. Sign it, seal it, and give this letter to your pre-teen when they have a low point. You may see yourself or your inner child within the hurting pre-teen in front of you. It will reassure them to know that you went through similar feelings, and you came out on the other side.

Teach Them "How-To" Treat You

You can't control what is said to you or how people interact with you. But if someone has something negative or unkind to say about themselves, it's up for us as fellow human beings not to lead them in that direction. When those somebodies are our own children, we better point out how they are treating themselves.

Parents need to be mindful that their children are the ones who will most likely carry on what they see modeled in the home through communication patterns as adults. If parents communicate with each other using judgmental criticisms or blaming statements, then there's a good chance this is what children will model too.

When our expectations for relationships don't align with reality, either because people don't live up to it or it's not realistic, frustration sets in and leads to anger and resentment over time. A better alternative is to show patience by giving ourselves positive affirmations:

- I am doing the very best that I can
- I am deeply loved and love being me
- I can be kind to myself and others
- I am always learning and growing
- I can pick myself up after I fall

Even before you communicate to others about how to treat you, you should know how to treat yourself and how you wish to be treated. This is one lesson that I learned a little late in life. If I had developed a practice of self-love and self-care earlier in my life, I would be 1000% more successful because I would have understood how to be resilient, how to refuel, and how be kind to myself and others. So, when I had a big failure, I could have bounced back faster. And I could have built my team and worked with people I liked and admired, opposed to people who just produced results. And I wouldn't have been so hard on myself for missing a deadline or not getting perfect results.

So much inspiration stems from loving yourself. As motivational speaker Lisa Nichols says, "How can we expect others to treat us better than we treat ourselves?"

The first time I heard her say that quote, it hit me square between the eyes with so much gravity. The lightbulb went on and I knew I was missing this recipe in my life. I realized that I didn't know how to treat myself with kindness and respect, so the negativity that stemmed from within overflowed into my relationships with others. The big discovery that I learned so late was the ability to refuel and heal myself.

In a world where self-care is not a priority and we are constantly told to "just do it," the need for self-love has never been more important. Social media makes it seem like everyone has perfect lives with no challenges or obstacles, but this couldn't be further from reality.

We are all human. We all have flaws and insecurities. These weaknesses are normal! It's okay to feel bad about yourself sometimes because that just means you're human! In fact, there might be some areas in your life right now that you don't want to admit, even to yourself. Maybe you've gained weight recently. Maybe you worry about the future. It's okay to feel that way. There will come a point when you can start caring for yourself. Remember to be kind and nurturing to your own self. Give yourself a break just as you would your child.

Self-care is a term that is often thrown around, but what does it really mean? It's important to take care of your mind and body so you can function at your best. You should treat yourself with love and respect to help you feel confident in who you are.

I used to treat myself with cheat meals, like a poutine or a gourmet pizza. Food was a love language in my Asian culture and in my family. But I realized that overeating isn't really care, it is indulgence. It took me a while to shift my mental perception about food. Then, I started investing in fitness classes, equipment, and activities as my reward. These items actually helped me care for my body. Those rewards turned into properly fitted clothing, after I lost 30 pounds. This new body was a nice reward. Even on my rest days, I visit a hot tub as a nice reward and a method for my self-care

If you know how to treat yourself with love and respect, you can teach others how to treat you and how to interact with you because you know what makes you feel good. Learn how to treat yourself with care, just because you value yourself and recognize that you are worth the effort.

3-PEAR CHALLENGES

There are many reasons why you may feel overwhelmed by your pre-teen's behavior, but it could be that they are just going through a stage that will right itself over time. As pre-teens develop new emotions, feelings, and thoughts, I want to clarify this little four-letter but powerful word that they may encounter. Love.

Before they go "Looking for Love in All the Wrong Places" as sung by country singer Johnny Lee, I want to break down the idea. It is important that they understand love before your pre-teens experience heartbreak. There are seven types of love that people look for, but we commonly mistake one type for the other. Clearly defining the various types of love helped me understand what love I was looking for or needed.

1. *Storge* love is unconditional kinship (Family Love)
2. *Ludus* love is playful and flirtatious (Attraction)
3. *Philia* love is an intimate friendship (Best Friends)
4. *Philautia* love is cared based self-esteem (Self-Love)
5. *Eros* love is a sexual passion (Romance or Lust)
6. *Pragma* love is longstanding respect (Commitment)
7. *Agape* love is a godly love for humanity (World Peace)

In my own experience as a pre-teen, I experienced several crushes, which were just puppy love. What was it that I wanted? Was it romance (*Eros*), a desire for intimacy (*Philia*), or just the enjoyment of hand holding and other public displays of affection (*Ludus*)? In hindsight, if I had more unconditional family love (*Storge*) and more self-care or love for myself (*Philautia*), I don't think I would have been so heartbroken when these crushes were rebuffed.

Even as a pre-teen, I knew I was loved. And my dad's or mom's love still continues to fill me. If only I had taught myself how to love myself at that young age, I wouldn't have had to search so hard externally for what I know now internally. I encourage you to learn to *love thyself*.

These challenges are designed to purposefully bring you through an emotional rollercoaster. Rise, fall, twist and turn, no matter what ride you are on, I want you and your pre-teen to experience it together. Discover how you are your own rescuer and how to call on each other if there is ever a need for a first responder.

CHALLENGE #1 - Watch a Moving Documentary

Introduce and watch with your pre-teen a real-life short or documentary of someone overcoming a trauma, challenge, or heartbreak. Pick one that moves you personally.

CHALLENGE #2 - How to Show and Receive Love

Look up the book, *The 5 Love Languages*, by Gary Chapman. Practice a different way of showing and giving love to your pre-teen. Try a new method for every day of the week. Determine which language your pre-teen responds to the most. Then, the following week, ask to receive love in all five ways from your pre-teen.

CHALLENGE #3 - Witness 10 Minutes of Self-Love

Create a practice of self-love and self-care. Invite your child to be present and observe for ten minutes of your practice. The only expectation is for your child to watch you because you want them to see you fill your internal well. If you struggle to find a practice, try standing in front of a mirror with yourself for ten minutes. Put a timer on and see what happens.

3-PAIR TAKEAWAYS

The Pre-Teen

It's not easy being a pre-teen. They're at the cusp of becoming adults, but they're still children. This age is when many kids experience their first heartbreak, yet they don't know how to handle it. We want our kids to be happy, but it's important to let them learn how to deal with hardship without giving up on themselves or others.

This age is a great time to build up their character. Traits such as resilience are developed as they build their self-esteem, self-confidence, and self-care. They have to do the work, but Dad, you get to show them how.

The First Responder

As your pre-teen's first responder, just follow these two simple steps: 1) Answer the call. 2) Show up. More than half your job is done through these practices.

The other 40% of parenting your pre-teen is just listening, and the care, empathy, and love they feel from you. Don't solve every problem for your children, just gather information and give them the space to feel out the issue and figure it out for themselves.

The last 10% contains your bag of tricks. Think of this portion as any missing piece of the puzzle. Give them hints, where to find answers, and how to turn the problem around. Then, watch in amazement as your pre-teen solves it.

The Pre-Teen and The First Responder

We have a tendency to focus on what's in front of us rather than looking below the surface for root causes of negative emotions. You have to go beneath the surface to understand why you feel hurt, worry, doubt, and even anger. Being aware of these causes can lead to significant changes in your life, as you see your true self more clearly.

Be your own rescuer.

PART II - GROWTH STAGES

During the Growth Stages, a person will face adversity, brave the elements, and explore their own development and growth. During these stages there can be lots of exposure to challenges and disappointment when children venture away from the nest of safety.

As a parent of grown children, our relationship focus changes from one of fiduciary and care-giving responsibilities to a more supportive and encouraging role that reinforces the foundation we built up in previous stages.

Dads, this is an opportunity for us to focus on our own development, setting an example for our loved ones to follow, your actions will remind your family that we always have room to grow and improve.

Chapter 5 - The Teen and The Shoulder

Teenagers are supposed to be in an anxious, rebellious phase of their lives, but what if your teen is just a jerk? It can be hard to tell when it's time to stop being the fun parent and start being the tough one. I work with parents whose teenagers seem like they're always mad at someone or something. They may even sometimes lash out at their parents for no apparent reason.

Perhaps you feel like you've tried everything - reasoning, punishments, rewards - and nothing has worked so far to connect with your teenager. Yet there are certain questions you need to ask yourself before giving up on your kid.

The first step is to remember what it was like to be in their shoes. What were you like as a teenager? What difficulties did you go through? Why did you feel rebellious or angry? Did you ever lash out uncontrollably? Maybe you still do!

Like most teenagers, I was filled with an attitude of independence, invincibility, and exemption from legal consequences during that period of my life. On top of that, the teenage brain and senses are heightened, like they are coming into their own power, similar to any superhero's origin story. With so much power comes not responsibility, but this sweet, sexy, luring forbidden fruit called temptation.

Teens want to test the limits of what they can accomplish in society, physically, mentally, and emotionally. Essentially, teens constantly test to discover where their boundaries are, how far they can bend the rules and push against their comfort zones.

As a teen, my conscience, my inner angel, was hogged-tied, gagged, and locked under a basement staircase while my inner devil rooted and cheered me on every adventure.

On one particular night, I was practicing my 15-year-old driving skills in a 1993 Honda civic hatchback that could be easily opened with a coat hanger. As a Boy Scout in the 90s, most of the gadgets, including cars, were simple circuits that could be easily bypassed, just like in the movies. Thanks, Knight Rider.

Driving was a new skill and thrilling ride. I'd had weeks of practice, so I was fairly good and speedy at handling the car. There was nothing like that feeling of cruising down the streets with the window rolled down and one arm out. It was that perfect mix of adrenaline and accomplishment. At 2 am there is a calm in the air, a stillness that makes you think you are the only one awake. You are the master of the universe and there are no consequences. But that feeling came crashing down with the flash of two distinct colors: red and blue.

Was I pulled over for driving too fast, or maybe because I was joying riding a stolen car, or maybe because I didn't have a license and was underage? Or maybe because I was reported missing, since I ran away from home two weeks earlier.

My new way of life in the Fast Lane ended with a backseat car ride to my parents' house. As a minor, I was legally still under their influence and care. I was escorted by the nice police officer up my driveway, as I felt my shoulders tighten, my gaze and head tilted towards the floor. I braced myself for the unleashing of yelling and punishment since I hadn't even seen them in a few weeks.

At that moment, I didn't know if my parents were tired or if they simply lost their minds. Instead of an angry verbal barrage, they calmly told me to go to my room. I marched upstairs, reluctantly wondering if they planned to send me to juvie jail or if they were going to kill me after the police left. This stoic approach was definitely not what I expected.

But as I opened the door to my room, the stale, teenage stench hit my nose, immediately telling me that nothing had been picked up, cleaned, or moved since I left two weeks earlier. The dust had collected on the desk and furniture in the room. It felt empty, devoid of love or care, abandoned almost.

I closed the door and slumped down on the shag carpet, barricading the door with my back, looking around the room. Still, in the middle of the night, the same glow from the streetlights outside illuminated my escape route. I sat in the stillness, listening to a voice inside my mind. "Are you sure you want to go back out there?"

Through the lens of my teenage mind, I had figured out how to be independent and it only took me two weeks to find the answers. For shelter, I couch-surfed in the homes of my new friends. For food, I went to the corner store. And for work, I sold stolen goods at the flea market. This independent life was all so alluring, way better than the nagging, scolding, and controlling environment of home. There seemed to be no real consequences. Just a car ride home. So, why didn't I go out that window when the coast was clear, and my parents were asleep again?

The reason I chose not to leave was certainty and safety. My parents created a margin of security. Home was a safe place to land after exploring, tripping, and making unlawful mistakes. Sure, living with my parents came with their stinking rules and constant negativity, but it was a place to fall back on, a net of safety for my high-flying adventures.

As a parent, I now understand the desire to keep my children safe. That need is a biological, hardwired strategy in most paternal relationships. You must ensure the survival of your species and kin. But no one tells you how to shoulder that burden, that worry. Nor are you trained for the extra depth needed to endure when your own flesh and blood breaks your heart.

The shoulder is what is needed to pair with this challenging stage of development. The shoulder is used to lean on, to carry weight, to take the brunt of a blow. The shoulder can also be used as a battering ram or to shield and turn away. As a parent, you will need both shoulders to do all these tasks and provide a safe space for your children.

Emotions High Means Intelligence Low

I am a fighter. I pick myself up and keep going, even when everything seems hopeless. I don't know how it is in your life but fighting back has been one of my solutions for as long as I can remember.

We all have moments when we feel hurt, scared, or anxious. The question is whether you will fight back when those feelings arise. Will you allow your fears and anxiety to cripple you? Or will you rise above them and be the person that you were created to be? That's up to you!

Every day, I meet with clients who struggle to find a way to fight back when they feel hurt or scared. Whether that issue is in their personal life, at work, or from an organization that was supposed to protect them, many people need help understanding what to do next when they feel defeated.

Many times, we don't know where the pain in our lives originates from. All we want is for someone else to fix it for us. It's hard enough getting up every day and putting on our "game face" without having all these other battles going on internally as well.

There are times when emotions are too hot, too powerful, and too wild. Poor choices often stem from actions taken when in a highly charged emotional state. When those emotions run high, the intelligence level stays low. Our ability to make wise decisions is often hindered in the heat of the moment. It is no one's job but our own to find a calmer, more mindful, and successful state.

When my wife and I met with a marriage counsellor, we used the phrase "flooded with emotions." We needed time for the waters to retreat and for the storm to calm. Naturally, I am a person with a high level of energy, and just a little surge or spike of energy or excitement can make those around me feel agitated. My up-and-down energy level and intensity was exhausting for my wife. Her favorite time was when I worked and focused my energy onto the keyboard so she could work beside me, reading her book. But when I cook, I am like a hurricane, juggling three burners and the oven. I litter the countertops with dirty dishes and taster spoons, listening to random 90s jams at a volume that could create shockwaves. I want to feel the music, the bass, the beat as I dance and cook in my eight-foot radius. She preferred me cooking quietly and calmly, cleaning as I followed the recipe, moving at the modest pace of a turtle.

These two states of energy have different purposes and need their place and time in my life and relationship. Likewise, much of the success in being a shoulder for your teenager is making sure one is available for them to lean on, and the other is turned away to give them the space to be independent and express themselves, without our prying eyes.

I think of my chef energy as the teenager, full of emotions, passion, and fire. I love the chaos and playing with my creative skills. My wife knows that it is dangerous in the kitchen with me and not to break my flow, especially when I am in the zone. The same energy is true with your teenager. They are going to need to use your good knife, break a dish, maybe burn their arm putting that dish in the oven. And if we take this metaphor out of the kitchen it may look like their first date, first car accident, even their job. It is your duty to shoulder them as they fall and need time to recover. Use the other shoulder to prop them up in celebration or to nudge them forward.

Shouldering that train wreck can be difficult, but how do you loosen the grip for control, or guidance, or authority? These great gifts are earned, not given. At this stage, you'll need to focus on removing the training wheels like you once did when they were toddlers. They need you there still, but the stakes are higher. Instead of a bike, they might learn to drive a car. Same scenario, different stakes. You need to also elevate the trust level between you and your teens. More responsibility means more trust needs to be developed. That trust is built by spending more quality time together. You can watch them and know that they will make good choice. They don't always have to be right or accident-free, but make sure they know when and how to ask for help.

Give your teens space to learn. Remember, you have two shoulders, and you will need to alternate between the supportive side and the side that turns away from them in trust. If they need a safe place to land, they will come and tap you on the shoulder for help.

3-PARE CHALLENGES

It's not easy watching someone you love suffering. It can be hard to know what to say or do for the best, especially when they're in a dark place. This is especially true with teenagers because they experience so many of these emotions for the first time which can make them feel quiet, charged, or intense.

But if you give them the space they need and respect their feelings, it will make a huge difference in their recovery time. When your loved one is ready, they may want to talk about what happened with you or others who care about them. But don't push them too hard to talk or to share. Just listen and do not judge. Keep your ears open and practice your breathing exercises to manage your own emotions. This practice will help you stay calm and collected.

Some parents act like teenagers because their own emotions are either too powerful, fresh, or just too hot to touch. These strong feelings might be a clue that we have some unresolved issues or displaced challenges in our own lives. Be mindful that just the slightest breeze or a single cigarette butt can spark a raging forest fire. And in an instant that flame can burn down all the trust, all relationships, the foundation that you have built between you and your teenager.

I like to imagine the scene from *Thor Ragnarök* when neither Thor nor Hulk are listening to each other. As they rub, sparks of rage and frustration create an inferno, and they lash out. Their disagreement becomes dangerously out of control for a brief moment but fizzles out quickly when one person decides not to dump anymore fuel on the fire.

Afterwards as they apologize, Hulk admits, "Hulk so angry, like fire. Thor like smoldering fire. Hulk like raging fire." We can learn so much from this super lesson because in the midst of an emotional moment, it's important to let the situation cool down and not put more fuel on the fire. Stop and get a breath of fresh air.

Fire is neutral, it is neither good nor bad. Fire can either be life-giving, keeping us warm and preventing us from freezing, or it can burn you up and turn you into ash. Treat your teenagers the way you would a fire. It is up to you to find the best distance from the flames and how to contain it safely. And yes, sometimes you may have to call on a first responder or fire fighter to help manage the flames.

Keep in mind that the fire isn't real, and you can remain unscathed by the heat and flames. There is a trick to staying in the path of the flames. Let it burn around you but don't let yourself be set on fire.

The challenges in this section are designed to keep any combustible materials away from the heat of emotions and to help eliminate the risk of an uncontrollable, raging forest fire. Dads, these methods will help us keep our cool, so we don't burn any bridges, relationships, or trust.

CHALLENGE #1 - Open Your Fingers

When you are in your emotional safe space together and the situation gets heated, you may feel yourself getting tense. Open your fingers and spread them apart like you are going to give a high five. When we get tense, our bodies subconsciously go into a fight-or-flight mode. Spreading your fingers is an easy technique that allows you to break the cycle of your biological reflex response. Opening your fingers will help the tension flow through your body rather than holding, restricting, or constricting that negative energy.

CHALLENGE #2 - Dive into the Emotional Cone

Plutchik's Wheel of Emotions is a great foundation for understanding our feelings and their polarized relationships with one another. As you dive deeper into this work, Plutchik's wheel and petals fold into a 3-D cone shape of emotions.

Our most intense emotions and easiest related behaviours sit at the top of the cone. But underneath those intense reactions are their emotional causes. Look at the example of the Hulk and Thor in the movie *Ragnarök* again. Underneath the rage and fire, the Hulk felt there was lack of acceptance. Sadness and remorse were the reasons for Thor's anger. Identify any low-intensity emotions associated with the large, more intense feelings that may hide what you truly feel.

CHALLENGE #3 - Forgive to Heal

This internal exercise and mental challenge can be used by both the teenager and parent. Most external conflicts involve another person. Whomever you are in conflict with or whatever the conflict, I want you to imagine a specific scenario, where the two of you could resolve your differences, argument, and conflict.

Even imaginary scenarios can be useful. Perhaps you imagine that a meteor destroyed Earth and everyone on it. Years later, when you see your adversary at a bar on Mars, would you strike up a conversation or buy that person a drink? Even as one of the last humans alive?

Creating even a single scenario where healing or a resolution is possible is a place for the healing process to begin. Only with this mental flexibility is it possible for the release of emotion and space to heal that allows forgiveness to begin.

Build Your Safe Space on Three Conditions

You might automatically think of your home as the safe space for your teens. But there is a more important place for this space to exist in your relationship. I am speaking of an emotional safe space, where your teenager can share without fear of repercussions or judgment. A place to be just heard.

But how do you bite your tongue and just listen to your teenager?

This question is not an easy one to answer. As parents, we want our kids to listen to us because of their age or lack of life experience, but this tactic isn't always the best case. Our job as parents is not simply to provide information but also to help our children find the solutions that work for them. So, how do we learn when it's okay to speak up and when it's better just to listen?

I know firsthand that it can be frustrating when your child doesn't want to do what you want them to, but there are ways of communicating that will make both of you happier.

During a barbeque at a friend's house, I was shocked to hear her daughter talk about her night out in explicit and intimate details. At first, I was on fire, ready and wanting to jump in to offer advice or sympathize. But I took my friend's lead and stopped myself from speaking out. It hit me that this was one of those moments when you have to bite your tongue and just listen. You have to put on your best poker face.

The teenager finished sharing and dropped off a bunch of red flags and concerns that warranted a call to the police. But after all that raw sharing, she said, "Thanks for listening, Mom." Then she walked out and carried on. I was mortified with the calm demeanour and poise of my friend. She turned to me and said, "That was hard as shit, but I'd rather know these details, Alfie. I'd rather her come to me than hide it or feel like no one cares, that no one is there to listen."

We carried on with the barbeque, but that nonchalant statement and explanation stuck with me. Her wisdom planted in my mind as a best practice. I felt so privileged to witness that interaction between mom and teenage daughter, and how they created an emotionally safe space. My friend didn't react like my parents would have. My parents would have grounded me, locked me in a room, and told me not to hang around those people anymore.

My recommendation is for every parent to create one of these rare places of emotional safety. You may even want to create a physical representation of this space. Actress Jada Pinkett-Smith hosts a Red Table Talk, a place where three generations of women come together to have some real conversations for all of Facebook to see. Dads, I encourage you to create a physical space like Jada did, where you can have these listening sessions. It can be your favorite sofa chair, a lawn chair on the patio, or even a ride in the car. Notice that I recommended a seated position because some of the stuff you might hear will floor you. So be supported, comfortable, and find a place of Zen, to just be present and listen.

My mentor Lisa Nichols taught this concept of a safe space and solidified the idea for me. For years, I watched her and saw how she grew her company while raising her son Jelani. They practiced creating this emotional space with three simple conditions:

1. No judgment
2. No repercussions
3. Unconditional love

Now Jelani teaches this practice in his own company, called Motivating the Teen Spirit that he and his mom started. This process is life-changing, and I've seen first-hand how well it works, even with young children.

So, give your teens space and a place to drop their emotional baggage. This space gives you a chance to see if a situation is broken and to examine their emotions. Not fix, not repair, but to look at their teenage baggage. There is no expectation to take on their problems or do anything with their emotions. The emotional safe space is merely a place where an act of sharing can happen, without the intention of taking action.

As a male, I recognize that strong, primal urge to fix problems, and YES, fixing a problem is important and needed. But first, you need to properly assess and recognize that someone else's problem is NOT yours to FIX. It is your job to shoulder the concern and lift them up, NOT solve the issue for them. So, bite your lip and hold your tongue. Just sit with them, watching them dive into their hurt, their pain, their emotions, their darkness. Sit next to them, so they are not alone and know they have a place to be heard.

This emotional safe space is like a GLASS HOUSE. It takes a gigantic amount of trust to build and maintain it. The walls and foundation are extremely fragile and easily broken. And if it ever cracks, it is prone to shatter which can be extremely dangerous. So please, treat this safe space with the highest regard. A glass house is not something you want to repair, crack, or enter mindlessly.

Before entering this sacred and fruitful place with your teen, understand that it will take time to create and grow. The trust must come naturally, not be forced. You need to nurture that place of safety and give it the right conditions. Nurture the spirit, the love, the light, and the truth in order to give that place its spark. Your job is to create and protect the space, then make it known to your teen that this safe space exists.

3-PEAR CHALLENGES

One of the hardest issues a parent has to face is helping their teen through difficult challenges. There are many times when you want to take on the burden for them and solve it for them, but becoming an adult is about learning how to become independent from your parents.

As your teenagers grow up, you want them to grow close to you, not further apart. So, what can we grow together, that will strengthen the bond between parent and child?

The following challenges are designed to strengthen the physical and emotional bond with activities that involve trust, vulnerability, discovery, and time.

CHALLENGE #1 - The Trust Carry

Dads, this physical challenge was specifically built for you. Do you remember when your teenager was a baby, and you carried them in your arms? Well today, they might be a little too big for that. But the act of being carried, and the deep emotions associated with that weightlessness and closeness is something that we become less familiar with.

The challenge is to build up to carrying your child again. Either a fireman carry, piggy-back, or a low-intensity shoulder hold and hug. This exercise is one to tack onto the end of a workout, which I recommend that you do together. Whether it is after a run, a hike, or a fitness classes you take together, try out this challenge.

Lifting your child will subliminally bring back a familiar, rooted nostalgia, where trust and love are expressed physically. Yet you can disguise it as a safety exercise.

You can always use the cover story, "What happens if you pass out and I have to carry you to the car or hospital, or out of the forest on your hike? Indulge your old man and see if he can still carry you to safety."

If you want to take this challenge a step further, place your trust in your teen. Do a role reversal and let them carry you. The ways you grow and maintain love with this exercise is through quality time and touch.

CHALLENGE #2 - Establish the Safe Space

We have talked about the importance of an emotional safe space. Create a physical location or anchor for this exchange to take place. For Jada Pinkett-Smith, her family talks happen around a red table. In our house that safe-space conversation happens over a placemat at our table, with our three rules of engagement written out in a way my young children can relate to.

1. Just Talking (No judgment)
2. No Time Outs (No repercussions)
3. More Hugs and Love (Unconditional love)

There is something about having these rules laid out, almost like a contract, so that trust can be built. I encourage you to add your own rules to engage in an emotional safe space and conversation. Develop these with your teenager.

Have your rules of the safe space printed on a wallet-sized card, personalized mug, or a keychain and give the item to your teenager as a gift and as an invitation. Let them know that you are always open to having and holding that space.

The way of showing and fostering your love for your teen is also grown with words of affirmation and combining it with a small, physical gift.

CHALLENGE #3 - Know your Emotional A.R.C.

This challenge takes a high level of self-awareness and time to adopt. It is a framework to understand one's emotions, reactions, and behaviours.

It is called "ARC of Emotions" for short.

- A = Antecedents (what happened before?)
- R = Response (your thoughts, feelings, and behaviours)
- C = Consequences (what happened next?)

You don't have to make your teenager fill out this form every time they have a meltdown or are feeling overwhelmed. But you can do them a big service by planting this process as a framework to follow. Or go-to methodology for understanding their emotions and how they react to them, and what becomes of a situation.

This tool is for assessment and monitoring. No solutions are given. It is simply a chance for your teen to frame and understand themselves better. It allows them to see patterns of how they react in different circumstances.

Incorporate the ARC in your conversation or use it as a guide to frame your leading questions with your child.

3-PAIR TAKEAWAYS

The Teen

The teen years are a time of great change, growth, and independence. This age is an exciting time when children start to explore their own identities and the world around them: their friends, schoolwork, peer pressure, and their future goals.

We know that teens are often moody and may have a hard time expressing their thoughts and feelings, but as dads, we want to know what is going on inside their heads and hearts.

One thing is for sure, there's so much more than just hormones raging. You have to take the time to figure out who your child is in this world and what kind of person he or she is becoming.

The Shoulder

Parenting a teen can be both fun and challenging at the same time. There are days when your son or daughter is so good that you want to give them credit for being "perfect," while there are other days when they are on their own little island of independence, raging against every boundary.

This is a turbulent time for parents as they struggle with understanding how best to guide their child through this period of life without losing connection or control. In most cases, you will have to shoulder and burden their fury, rage, and their displaced emotions without trying to fix their problems.

The Teen and The Shoulder

The relationship between parents and their teenage children can be difficult, but it doesn't have to be. Here are my three simple tips for dads for keeping and strengthening this relationship:

1) Focus on building trust. Make clear agreements.
2) Create an emotionally safe space. Share and listen.
3) Remember to use your shoulders. Turn away from taking over but invite them to come to you when needed.

Remember, the goal is for your teen to grow into adulthood, but they will have to do this by themselves. So, give them the physical room they need to figure it out on their own. Turn your shoulder but keep that space and line of communication open.

<u>Chapter 6 - The Young Adult and the Communicator</u>

Leaving the high-school world of secondary education is a scary reality. There is no longer a standard path to follow. As a young adult, how do you know what you want to do? How do you know where you want to commit your money, education, or efforts for the rest of your life?

If you are an Asian child, your parents have probably spelled out the expected path for you. This course is usually based on their unfinished dreams, their hopes, or their secret wishes for their own lives. Whether they want their children to be doctors, accountants, pharmacists, teachers, or civic workers, the choice is usually based in fear, safety, and a familiar route. Most Asian parents promote, seed, and implant these career choices into their children.

It was never really clear what my path was supposed to be. When my parents left Hong Kong and Macau, China, they had dreams of a better future, a more prosperous one, and a new life in Canada. My father was a successful TV station producer and my mother a talented business accountant. They both were ambitious and knew they could find more opportunities in North America and live a more prosperous life.

My mom and dad searched for work on their way from the frigid east side of Canada to the warmer west coast of Vancouver. As they broke ground in this foreign, frozen land, their internal fire and dreams started to freeze and die out. Their ambition turned into survival, with their familial safety net over 15,000 kilometers away on another continent. They only had each other to look to for support, especially since English was their second language.

Regardless of their English skills, my dad found that he could work as a cook which didn't require significant language skills. Since he had worked in film in Asia, he knew how to produce on demand and conduct himself in harmony with a team. He easily caught on to the demands of a kitchen. He quickly worked his way up from line cook on the railroads, to sous chef in banquet halls, to head chef at some of Vancouver's largest hotel chains.

My mother also had her challenges. Her shortest career lasted only one day. As a full-serve gas attendant who was only 5 foot, 2 inches tall, she couldn't reach across the windshields of the jacked-up trucks of Alberta. Her search to better match her skills and talents led her to accounting. She didn't really need to speak fluently to crunch numbers. She found work as an accounting clerk at DHL Worldwide Express, a shipping company. She knew the world of shipping and delivery since she grew up in a family who traded with the Western world at the many ports of Hong Kong. My mother always bragged about her dad, who was the only one in her town who wore a western three-piece suit, as opposed to a traditional silk Chinese outfit. These suits represented opportunity and growth for my family, and they left such an impression on my mom as a young adult, she left the East and headed west in search for her own fortune and opportunities.

As my parents immigrated to North America, and started a brand-new life, in this foreign land, I can't help but wonder what their hopes and dreams were. Were they looking for the Hollywood movie experience, or for opportunities to do business and trade internationally? Instead, they settled in regular, middle-income jobs in accounting and cuisine.

I feel there is an unspoken brokenness and regret that is imprinted on all youth born to immigrant parents. We watch our parents struggle with language and hurdle over certification requirements, climbing mountains to fit in to a culture not like their own, with very little support around them.

I grew up with very few family members or cousins near us. My closest family influences were three cousins who lived six hours away in Portland, Oregon. Their dad, my mom's older brother, was a successful dentist who berated me mentally with his demands to, "Study first," and "Dumb, you dumb." Still to this day, I really don't know what the second phrase means, but I knew I wanted to avoid hearing it. That desire to avoid confrontations with him was motivation enough to study first.

So, I buried myself in the academic world, first earning a college leadership diploma, then a tourism and recreation degree while going to film school. Nearly six years of post-secondary education helped prolong my entry into the grown-up world of work. And per my family instructions, I just stock-piled one academic credential after the other. With each graduation ceremony, I waited for something magical to happen, for the gates of career opportunities to open, for the dream acting role to appear out of the blue, or the venture capital money to appear and fund a tourism company. I did what my parents and family told me to do. I got a good education, but I wasn't sure when or how the payoffs would come.

Naturally after film school, I pursued my art, but I was also practical and took a government job as a safety net. These jobs provided a great balance. My government boss was a dance mom and understood about supporting art while being practical and earning a living. She gave me a balance of part-time work and the freedom to pursue my artistic talents. I was a "parallel-prenuer," working two simultaneous careers. But that dream came to head one day when my boss offered me full-time employment. This kind of opportunity didn't come around very often. It was the fork in the road between what was a certain path with government work versus the other path that was the artist's way. At the time, it felt like a I had to make a major decision.

That evening, I sat at my round dining table where I had sat a thousand times, looking for direction, guidance. But that day, the stone table was cold to the touch. As my internal burden placed all its weight on it, the table did not offer any warmth or comfort. The cold stone just added to the heaviness on my heart. I was stunted by my fog of emotion, struggling to bring forth words to describe my pain and dilemma. A war waged between my heart and my head. My heart screamed at me to stay on the artist's path. It was the one that felt right and would bring me true joy and fulfillment. I was built for the road less traveled.

But at the same time, my head argued logically that this full-time position would secure a lifestyle, a known future, and an assured path of success for my desires. The job would provide rewards I could count on with guaranteed outcomes, laid out in a secure path with a definitive timeline. The decision on what path to take was like a tug of war between my heart and head, which ripped apart my certainty, clarity, and vision.

My mind battled to claim victory, as my heart tried to cry out, pleading for the advice of my artistic friends to turn the tide. But no hero was called up, no rescue happened, no cavalry appeared at the top of the hill. The sun set on the dream of the artistic path.

In body and mind, I accepted the full-time position with the government which put the nail in the coffin of my heart's artist chapter. My logical mind won a victory that day which governed me for almost 20 years. This choice was a failure to truly communicate what my heart asked for. But its pleas were not heard, nor were they strong enough to stand up and communicate clearly to my dominant mind.

I don't regret the decision to journey with my mind's plan; that path created many benefits and provided me security. I got major promotions, paid off student loans, bought my first brand-new car, and built my dream property. But by operating solely from my mind's instructions, I squashed the voice of my soul and heart. The cries of emotions or inner desires were silenced in the pursuit of these mental success goal posts.

Embrace the "NO's" Before Finding "Yes"

We all want to be liked and accepted. We can't even imagine what it's like not having friends or a family that cares about us. So, when someone asks for a favor, we often say yes. The problem is that this one small word often leads to over-commitment which leaves us feeling resentful and overwhelmed. What saying yes does is take away time, energy, and resources for the activities that we want to do or objects we desire.

The word NO is not a bad word. Saying no can lead to a better life. In order to say yes to what we truly desire, we have to learn how to say no first.

I need a constant reminder of this truth. Warren Buffett, one of the world's best investors, developed a great method to focus on the power of the NO. Buffett got this method from his mentor Benjamin Graham who encouraged Buffet to focus on 20 companies that he wanted to love and know deeply. He grew rich trading and investing in those companies. All you need is four or five companies to get rich and be successful investor.

Make a list of all the things you want to do, then choose five that you'll commit to. Get rid the other items from your list until you accomplish your top five choices. Get to your NO faster.

My concept of paring and pruning areas of your life came from this idea. I wasn't blessed with a path that was tread, set, or marked. I was given a finicky compass, sensitive to items with a strong magnetic force. I got sucked into shiny endeavours, paths with promises to greatness, and even red-carpet challenges.

As a young adult, I started down the path of many diverse careers: the performing arts, recreation and tourism, financial advising and services, and a practical government job in digital and community services with a strong focus on corporate education.

I wasn't aware of why I was motivated to search and explore so many paths. But I what I found was the momentum and conviction that staying along that path wasn't for me.

I missed my friends' weddings because of my commitment demands of the stage – one or two shows per day, seven days a week. I knew after my commitment to the theatre I wanted the freedom to control my time. Yet I was lured by the stage and screen, the fame, the accolades, the euphoric lifestyle, the care and comradery. In the acting industry, we worked together, played together, and even ate together. This field treats their employees as people, caring for basic needs, and nurturing them. In certain organizations that I have belonged to, I was spoiled with a very high level of care and nutrition to promote health. Those in the movie industry know the lure of the craft services or even the lunch truck.

But sometimes, you have to give up and say NO. Not just to the free food, but also the promises of fame or fortune, the search for bliss, or an easy life, surrounded by artists and fun, engaging people. Life on a movie set, where food, shelter, and a common goal are directed, is easy. Real life does quite operate the same way. We have to direct our own lives, write our own scripts, and set our own accomplishments.

I made a hard choice to put down the dreams and pick a different path that my heart and soul led me towards. A path of reality, of learning that life isn't always rainbows, unicorns, sunshine, and cupcakes. I chose a real existence with up and downs, not a smooth, utopian experience. I decided to say NO to the fantasy and walk a path of reality. At the time, I didn't realize that I was walking away from a dream that no longer served me or grew me.

We must learn to let go of those activities and dreams that no longer serve us, without guilt or regret. Yet it is important, not just to move on, but to take the time to mourn and say goodbye to those ideas with appreciation.

As young adults, you may find it difficult to navigate today's world of endless content and information, marketing and messages. I encourage you to spend some time away from your devices and the internet, away from the busy workplace or bustling city. Go somewhere quiet, where you can listen to yourself, your heart, your mind, and your soul. Give each voice a space to deliver its message to you.

As parents of these bright-eyed, young-adult explorers, we can still provide a physical space and quality time to prompt those open-ended questions concerning our children's career journey, their highs and lows of the week, as well as any insights to life, passion, or calling. Encourage sharing and ask permission to share your own life experiences and lessons from similar situations.

3-PARE CHALLENGES

When parents finally accept that their children are leaving the nest, they must detach themselves. To make this emotional transition easier on both parties involved, most young adults subconsciously try to sabotage their relationships with their parents. They set out to prove wrong those who were supposed to be infallible and right about everything when it came down to parenting advice. They may even offer advice about parenting to their own fathers and mothers.

They eventually try to prove themselves right by leaving for good without coming back. This break from supportive ties may leave them depressed or unconnected so that it is more difficult to recover from setbacks.

There are countless ways that we can stop ourselves from growing, and the realization is hard to swallow. However, paring beliefs and habits that don't serve you can ultimately be liberating and empowering. In order to make big changes in your life, you've got to be willing to cut out the areas that hold you back.

As a parent of a young adult, there is a good chance that your young adult-child will take up residence in your home again. If they do return, it means that you created a safe space for them to fly, fail, and land.

Give them the runway to take off again by maintaining open lines of communication and understanding with them so that the relationship can continue to grow.

And if your young adult children aren't in your safe space or physically in your home, reach out. Remember to:

- Have their back. Be supportive of their choices, even if you don't agree with what they've done.

- Be honest. Be upfront about how you feel but don't criticize or judge their choices.
- Give space. Give them time to do activities on their own without interference from parents

These pare challenges are designed to identify the words we say that don't serve us and the pursuits that suck up our time. We need to know what steals our belief or focus, so we can build up ourselves and the areas that truly matter in our lives.

Less is more. — Ludwig Wies van der Rohe (Architect)

Challenge #1 - Know Your Lies.

Grab a pencil and a pen. What do you say to yourself that is negative? Do a free write, jot down whatever comes to mind on your paper, the good, the bad and the ugly. Do this challenge, especially when you have a rough day, tough time, or are in the depth of depression. Write down in pencil what the little voice inside your head says to you. This list is a LIE. Replace the first thought with positive, true statement in pen. Then scratch out or erase the LIE.

~~LIE: I am not a success until I buy my own house.~~

TRUTH: My success includes more than just owning a house.

TRUTH: Homeownership does not define my success.

TRUTH: I am successful because I am…

TRUTH: I define my true success as…

Write down enough truth statements until you find one that you believe in and that you know to be true. This exercise helps you replace those negative thoughts with your own empowering message.

Challenge #2 - Cut the List

For young adults, there are so many goals or desires we want for ourselves in dating, careers, or fitness. Make a list of all these mental, social, or emotional wishes for yourself. Do not limit your list. Write everything down.

After you dump all your thoughts out on paper, start to identify the areas of your life you want to focus on. You can categorize your wishes to into three categories including, physical/material goals, mental/internal goals, and spiritual/connection goals.

For a balanced approach, I suggest choosing at least one goal from each of these categories (three in total) to focus your effort on. Move all the other wishes and desires onto the "avoid list." Post both lists side-by-side in your office or on your desk, so you know what to focus on and what desires you need to sideline until you accomplish your top three goals.

Challenge #3 - "Do You K(NO)w how They Did It?"

Reach out and interview a successful person in your career field and learn about their path. Take them for coffee or set up a Zoom meeting, then listen to their rules and recipe for success. List qualities that make them great at their career. Ask them what they had to say NO to and how they deny themselves in order to be successful.

Read the Body, Find the Truth!

We all start with the same potential and there are many opportunities in the world. The problem is not that there are not enough opportunities, but rather people think they cannot see or hear them.

Why do so many people fail when they have the opportunity for success? Our culture expects that we should always be able to do anything we want. The problem with this mindset is that it sets up unrealistic expectations. We can't always have whatever we want, and often the shared benefits don't include the true costs of achieving them.

Sometimes, we are not ready for life's challenges. We get carried away with the benefits and forget about the rest. We need to set time aside to think about our life decisions.

We make decisions too fast. Sometimes we do this because we are told to by ads and commercials that it's too easy to order our desires online. We need to continue practicing that lesson where we take our time to make decisions instead of rushing into them.

The key to that lesson is the skill of discernment. Discernment is one tool that will help you make more informed decisions about your life and your future. Discernment does not mean judging or making quick conclusions without knowing all the facts. Instead, it allows you to sense when there is an issue or problem so you can take action. Discernment allows you to formulate your own thoughts and measures, not accepting information at face value or at a surface level.

Discernment takes you to a deeper level of listening, understanding, and questioning. It goes beyond just reading between the lines, because discernment also applies to your message and your intentions.

You are constantly communicating, even when you do not say anything. Studies show that over 55% percent of communication is said through body language, nearly 40% is based on the tone of your voice, and just 5% of what is communicated happens through words. So, it is vital for you to discern what others' body language says, or even what mood, tone, or vibes that person's gives off.

Keeping lines of communication open is so important for clarifying our circumstances. Communicating face-to-face will give us a clearer sense of the full message being sent.

We cannot always talk freely and vulnerably around certain people. I learnt the hard way that not every private conversation stays between friends, nor is it protocol to honor privacy, especially under pressure.

The biggest lesson I learnt is that you should think about what you say before you say it. You never know how people will react to what you said. They will take away, not just your words from a conversation, but also their feelings about what you said. They might even use your words against you later on. Just one sound bite can change your life's course.

My words took me on a trip to the looney bin because of my honest answers and reply. Under my policy that truth is always the best, there were others smart and cunning enough to elicit a phrase, a position, and an interpretation on the record to use against me. So, when I spoke my truth, it got me locked up and admitted to the psych ward for over 48 hours, just before my daughter's birthday.

I was locked up when I told the truth about my feelings. But my honest communication also got me out in the end. All of my accusers' stories or pictures couldn't be ignored in the light of my honesty. Deceitful people may use my honesty against me. They may take what I say in confidence and use it against me. I hope you never have to deal with someone like this. But if you do, I hope you learn how to stay authentic and true to yourself. Know that being honest and true to yourself will always bring you freedom.

Stand in your truth and trust in your body to help communicate your message, even if you don't have the words.

3-PEAR CHALLENGES

Today's young adults are faced with unlimited options and presented with endless opportunity through the glass screen of their devices. They have no idea what they want to be, who they want to marry, where they want to live, or how many kids they will have. The one skill that is needed more than any other for young people in this environment is discernment.

As parents, we want to provide our children with the best of everything. We want them to have a good education, be well fed, and have their own home. But sometimes, these physical provisions are not enough, and they may become unhappy or rebellious.

If you notice your adult child is struggling financially, has health problems, or experiences marital strife, that is a sign that you may not be maintaining a close enough relationship with them.

Be there for your adult children when circumstances get tough. Sometimes, they just need someone who will listen without judgment and offer support when needed. This assistance should come from family members first. But if there is a family rift, then reach out to your family management team, the board of directors comprised of friends and professionals that they surround themselves with.

These next challenges are designed for parents and their children to practice together as they learn the skills of listening, setting your own inner voice, and receiving trusted and honest feedback.

CHALLENGE #1 - Five-Minute Share.

With this challenge there is one person (parent) speaking and one person (young adult) listening. Position yourselves shoulder to shoulder - not across from one another. Being side-by-side sends a physiological message to each person that they are on the same side.

The speaker will just share for five minutes; set a timer if needed. The only standard response is, "Thank you for sharing." Then switch roles and have your young adult share. After their five minutes, the parent will repeat the standard response, "Thank you for sharing."

This challenged is designed to get a conversation started as a trust-building exercise that ensure that each person can share completely, without interruption. The sharer is guaranteed a safe and expected response.

CHALLENGE #2 - Mission statement.

Think about what you want to tell yourself every day. Or better yet, consider what you need to tell yourself every day. The affirmations talked about in the chapter on teenage years are about our values, what we stand for, and what we care about. Finding a mission statement, however, is a little different than an affirmation.

A mission statement is typically future-focused. A mission statement determines what you want to do or accomplish, and how you want circumstances to unfold.

- To create a…
- To become the…
- To help…

This book's mission statement is "to help raise Emotionally Healthy Children and have them become Wildly Wealthy Adults" As you decide what you want to achieve and what goals are most important to you, create your own mission statement, including what you want to do, how, and why.

This exercise anchors our easily distracted minds and brings focus to our intentions. We need an active and purposeful filter that brings our interests to the forefront of our minds.

CHALLENGE #3 - Honest Feedback

Find a trusted source or an established communication partner. If you have trust, respect, and deep honesty with this person, elicit some feedback and brutally honest criticism.

Ask the question. "What do I need to focus on or see that I might not be aware of?"

The goal of this powerful and sensitive questions is to bring into your vision a problem area that maybe in your blind spot. Your trusted friend will help bring this concern to light. Their honesty will probably sting or trigger an emotional response. But just like the first challenge, a genuine and standard response to this honesty is, "Thank you for sharing."

This last exercise helps us all to receive a message that may be emotionally triggered or sensitive. But by proactively asking for this honesty, you set the conditions and the time when you are open to receive it. Remember, if you are not open to it, do not do this exercise. You have to be open and willing to hear their opinions.

And then you can discern if their point is true for you or not. You choose how to react, behave, and respond to that information.

Our methods of communication are changing, evolving, and advancing. The communication norms, the tools, the etiquette, the social channels, the media platforms. But the basic structure in quality communication remains the same. First you SHARE, then you LISTEN, and then CONFIRM the message.

3-PAIR TAKEAWAYS

The Young Adult

There are many pressures in today's society for young adults to say yes to everything, but I am here to tell you that saying no sometimes can lead to a better life.

There is no need for guilt or shame when it comes time to turn down an invitation because of busy schedules and responsibilities. With the right mindset, saying no can be more freeing and allow space to find that true "yes."

The Communicator

All parents want to have a strong relationship with their children. Sometimes that takes more effort than others, especially in the case of young adult children. It can be a difficult transition for parents to suddenly not have their kids around them all the time anymore. The fear of losing our children in some way is often pervasive throughout this stage of parenting as well.

This feeling is why I stress the importance of communication, quality communication. Be the place where your children can have a safe, open, honest conversation. A place to practice receiving feedback in the most loving, heartfelt, and constructive way. Your children need to learn how to process information that is difficult or unpleasant to hear.

Be present and compassionate in your communication. Be the favorite place to share, be heard, and be celebrated. Then your children will come back for more, even after they leave the nest.

The Young Adult and The Communicator

Throughout the growth stages, our children listened to us, taking our direction and advice as we guided their development. But as young adults, they will have to discern their own life's mission and purpose.

We can help equip them with the tools to search and find that purpose on their own. The best tool you can give them is to show them how to communicate. Develop your young adults' ability to listen, share, and give or receive feedback.

As a strong communicator, you'll have a clear relationship with each other, and most importantly, with yourself.

<u>Chapter 7 - The Adult and The Engineer</u>

Do you ever wonder what your child's future will be like? What are their dreams? How do they plan to make those dreams happen? What if there is another global pandemic? Will they be able to find a job or make money?

The world is changing rapidly. Technology is advancing at an unprecedented rate. The landscape of the business world has shifted from a manufacturing and production-based economy to one that relies on knowledge, creativity, and innovation. What does this evolution mean for your children? Our children need to start preparing now for a very different future than we experienced.

How can we help them prepare for a future when machines perform more and more tasks, technology dominates everyday life, jobs are scarce or require advanced technical skills, and high unemployment rates mean more competition?

The world is a scary place. It's full of uncertainty and there are many unknown hazards that we may face in the future. When I feel anxious or uncertain about my life, I try to step back and get perspective on the situation by asking myself these five questions:

1. What part of this situation am I responsible for?
2. What can I learn from this experience?
3. Am I doing anything to help myself feel better?
4. How will this worry affect those around me if they see me reacting in a negative way?
5. Does what is happening now have any effect on my life over the long-term?

My adult experience has always involved planning and reverse engineering the design of my future. I learnt the manifestation technique of visualization and the Law of Attraction from a documentary called *The Secret.* This film featured personal-development guru John Assaraf. He explained how he used vision boards to manifest his desires. He cut out photos, magazine articles, titles, and pictures, then pasted them together on a 24" x 36" foamboard. A few short years later, while moving into his new home and office, he unpacked a box with of his vision board. And without realizing it, he had moved into the exact house he pasted on his board years before.

I decided if manifesting worked for John, maybe it would work for me too. At the centre of my 2014 vision board was "The Happy Family Formula" with images of floor plans and designs for my perfect dream home. It also included a perfect marriage, rooms for my unborn children and a house in the back for my aging parents. On my board I built up the property to be a multigenerational utopia and the foundation for my dreams and legacy.

This million-dollar, corner-lot estate in the City, with a custom-built coach house had everything except the white picket fence. *The*

Secret was right; whatever I put on my vision board would come to life. I could manifest my dreams.

But what did that dream cost me? I busted my butt looking to provide a happy life for my wife. My mission statement was, "Happy wife, happy life." I worked a 7am to 5 pm job, while upgrading my skills with certifications and credentials. I made bets on speculative investments that I hoped would pay off big. I kept grinding at a side hustle in network marketing and took on any film opportunities I could find. Every ounce of my energy and hustle was spent manifesting my dream home and dream life. I pushed forward, down the long road called success, looking for my big break.

Well, a big break is what exactly what I got one week in the middle of March 2018. After performing corporate training for seven years, teaching over 40 different software programs, nine hours each day to hundreds of students, I had nothing to show but five failed job interviews for any higher positions. The hiring committee told me that I was passed over due to certification, not job experience.

Crushed, I headed to my car to gather my pride, my precious papers, and my tears. Then, I lifted my head and put a smile back on so I could face my students and teach them how to find success along this corporate journey.

The next day, as I came back to my dream home, I got a knock on the window. "Are you Mr. Alfred Liu? You have been served." Then, the nice gentlemen just walked away. He left me with official court documents saying my contractor was suing me.

Friday, I got a phone call that my aunt passed away. My parents faced so much death of family and friends. My aunt was the fifth loss in just a single year.

Saturday, I was forced to decide if I wanted to reup an investment in an inventory and marketing firm. It was a hefty price tag for a struggling business under a year old. I felt like this rocket ship business would never leave the ground. I was just bleeding chips as my money drained away, without a proof of concept or any guarantees.

On Sunday, my wife's water broke, and it was time for the birth of my second child. My wife and I already had a healthy little girl, who had her gender reveal cake, team pink. For this baby, I wanted to keep the sex a surprise. I just knew this time that my wife would surprise me with a baby boy, a coveted choice in most Asian families. Instead, we welcomed our second baby girl.

Late that night, with a newborn baby girl and a young toddler, my thoughts lingered on all my failures. At 3am, with only 20 hours of sleep the entire week, I wondered what else could go wrong. And I BROKE.

I no longer knew what I thought or felt. The world seemed to go dark. All I could do was go into a lifeless, soulless, zombie-like action. It was a mode that I was familiar operating in. Previously, I just pushed forward, stumbling until I got back on my feet.

But this time, the darkness was different. It had been several decades since I had thoughts of suicide, self-harm, or even harm to others. But something inside of my mind cracked, and my heart felt broken. My life was like a frayed power cord that was soaked in water. In a quick flash, I short circuited. I was still attached to the outlet but felt lifeless, dead, with no power. I just watched the world as it happened around me. The fire for life, the passion, the drive, and the thirst were no longer there. A third-person operation took place, and I was removed from all feeling and pain, simply going through the prescribed motions.

I didn't even care what others thought. I was distracted, weighed down by my baggage. Life was muted by all the hurt and pain. I felt like Bruce Banner turning involuntarily into the Hulk, out of control, and in the passenger seat. Like him, I wanted to smash everything to bits, including my pain, hurt, and sorrow.

Even as the Hulk shook my world and tore down buildings, the cornerstones and the foundations remained. All my visions, all my designs, all my ambitions, all my dreams lay crushed, dashed, and destroyed. The vision board, and its manifestation tools were powerful, but I came to understand that as the engineer of my life, my job isn't to be the master visionary or to design a wonderful piece of art.

An engineer's goal is to ensure that the plan is built to code, that the structure has integrity, that the foundation can withstand a certain load. As the engineer for your family and growing adult, make sure you plan for a disaster. Dads with adult children, did you plan for a global pandemic that lasted over a year? Did your children come back home? Did they lose their jobs? Did they get sick?

We must build an infrastructure that supports whatever comes our way. This foundation may include an emergency fund, extra rooms, or generating enough income to support the rest of your family.

An engineer of a family must ask the right questions. They must know if they can handle the load or build something that can support that load even under a stress test.

Build to last, build to support, build to withstand, build to succeed. Build to your own specs. Engineer your life.

Payment Due: 40 Minutes Per Day

Do you ever find yourself saying there isn't enough time? You are not alone. In fact, this is the number one excuse people use for not doing what they want to do in life or work. If there is a strong enough need, we will always find time.

Just think about the time you got a flat tire, your water tank burst, or you refinanced your mortgage. Where did you find the time to fix the problem? You made the time. You deemed the situation as important, so you found the time.

Time is a resource that we cannot gather more of. So, prioritizing your time can be very powerful tool and lesson. Most of us, never see the benefit of dedicating small increments of time to reach a goal or outcome over a prolonged period of time. That consistency and dedication can give you tremendous, compounded results or returns over a long duration.

This concept is most evident in the investing world. Investors are obsessed with numbers and rates of return. We know firsthand, how each miniscule percentage adds up, day after day. And if we invest long enough, we see the amazing benefits and results of compounding our interest. Many different industries recognize the benefits and effects of compounding which produces incredible results over time.

This one concept from the investment world needs to be applied, not just to your portfolio, but to the business of your family, to your parenting, and your CEO vision and mission for your company.

Most people underestimate what they can accomplish in five years. But with 525,600 minutes every year, you can carve out a few minutes to pursue your dream. Statistics say that it takes 600,000 minutes to learn and master a single skill. That means if you have held a job for more than five years, you should be a master at your job.

It only takes 20 hours to become proficient at a skill, for utilitarian purposes, not a competitive or Olympic performance level. However, developing a proficient level for a new skill may allow you to develop a few side gigs.

If you commit yourself to at least a month dedicated to practicing, you can acquire a new skill with just 40 minutes a day. A daily routine or practice builds from repetition and consistency. With daily practice, you could learn a detailed skillset within a year and be decent at it.

Everything is easier in life, if we break the task down into manageable, bite-sized pieces that are doable. The important thing is to make the steps achievable as you leverage the momentum that you create with discipline. Remember that it takes about 20 hours to obtain the skill.

So, carve out the time for self-improvement by figuring out how many 40-minute blocks you can stack into each day. You'll be surprised at how your momentum makes the latter half of the practice easier.

Perhaps the reason your new skill doesn't come easily is because it takes time to sink into deep work. Most of us eventually dial into a focused or concentrated stage, but it takes about 20 minutes to reach that flow state.

But just like your favorite TV show is released at a specific time, imagine that your new skill time must happen every day at the same time, like when you wake up to brush your teeth. Make your practice a habit by building it into your routine.

Understanding and applying the power of time is a valuable tool. Consider how you can use this tool to fulfill your mission statement you created in the previous chapter. I dedicate my 40 minutes per day to be present with each of my children and my wife, listening, sharing, and connecting. I know the importance of investing in those three relationships that I cherish the most.

Allot 40 minutes of quality time per day to your own relationships so you can be truly present with the ones you love.

3-PARE CHALLENGES

We all have 24 hours in a day. Yet some of us say there's not enough time to do what we want to do. But that idea is just an excuse. We can always find the time if we really want something badly enough.

If you need to accomplish a task or fix a problem, you'll find the time if it's important to you and you're willing to make the effort. We all have 24 hours in a day, no matter what our priorities are.

Let's take on a few of these challenges to help us find the time. Focus on what your priorities are to discover what you want enough to make it happen.

The following challenges are about putting your intentions to paper and creating a plan to execute them, rather than just a mission statement. These challenges will help you carve out time, money, and the resources needed to fund your plan.

CHALLENGE #1 – Unplug and Create Downtime

Set time limits on your phone, digital devices, or the internet. Analyze your overall screen time. Look at the apps that you spend the most time on. Take a screenshot as a reminder and commit to reduce your overall screen time.

Make a goal to reduce your screen time by ten percent every month. Or you may want to set time limits on certain apps. Consider setting a digital fasting window when you don't use any internet service or device between 10pm to and 6am.

Here is how to access the monitoring features directly built into your phones and devices. They provide simple solutions to limiting internet usage.

- Apple devices: Settings -> Screen time -> Downtime
- Android devices: Settings -> Digital Wellbeing and Parental Controls -> Ways to Disconnect
- WIFI Router -> On/Off power button

CHALLENGE #2 – Start with the End in Mind

Breaking down the steps you need to complete on a project or goal is vital skill of the successful. To reverse engineer a project, I go through a three-phase process that includes Analysis, Remodelling, and Implementation.

- Analysis encompasses understanding the components of your project. Simplify, then categorize or break it down into three areas.
- Remodelling identifies all the action steps you need to take. To begin with, choose the top two action steps to take in each area.
- Implementation creates the schedule to complete one action step per day in 40-minutes blocks. Remember to take Sunday off to give yourself some rest and recovery, no matter what the goal is.

It is easy to waste so much time with meaningless tasks. Carve out time for what's important to your health and your relationships. This recommendation is especially true for parents who are getting older, and for adults navigating their careers, relationships, and households.

If you fail to plan, you are planning to fail! - Benjamin Franklin.

CHALLENGE #3 - Give Yourself Five

Set aside five percent of your income to allocate funds dedicated to helping you experience your dreams. This small amount should be spent on rewarding yourself, educating yourself, and investing in your growth.

Most people stop investing in themselves after college or school. They spend money on movies, entertainment, and events. But how much of that funding is budgeted toward items that help develop you as a father, as a husband, or as an entrepreneur.

Carve out some money to invest in your education your growth. As your adult children attend university or get their professional certifications, you too can continue your education. Investing in yourself is a safe bet and helps develop a wealthy mindset.

Put Your Subconscious to Work

When I became a parent, I learned that there are gears and levels to parenting. There is the easy gear, where you understand your child's needs and wants, with little to no effort on your part. Then there is the hard gear, where you feel completely drained by your child's constant demands for attention and care. But what about those gears in-between?

The biggest key to my secret gear setting is based on momentum energy. Most people who study energy know that an object in motion, like a bike or car, is easier to keep in motion than to constantly stop and start. The same principle applies to us humans.

If we are not derailed or distracted, we can build momentum in achieving our big goal or projects. This energy to accomplish our goals is multiplied and arranged to welcome other contributors, much like a rotary engine or a spinning top that just needs a slight flick to keep it spinning. A rocket in space takes a tremendous amount of energy to fight the forces of gravity, but once it surpasses the earth's atmosphere, it continues its weightless orbit with far less effort.

Rockets and space remind me of Elon Musk, CEO of Telsa Motors and owner of SpaceX, one of the most influential visionary leaders of our time. He demonstrates the power of a dream, and his brain is always working. What fuels him is his vision for a sustainable future for humanity.

I was first shown the technique of visualization by my mom who showed me the movie, *The Secret*. In the film,
Jon Assaraf explained how visualization worked in his own life as he manifested his dream home.

I have adopted visualization practices into my own life for the past several decades. When I feel unmotivated or unclear, usually the first place I go to is my notebook/ journal to highlight words, sentences, or ideas I jotted down. With those words implanted into my subconscious, I go to a library or bookstore where there are lots of magazine or images I can flip through with my hands. There is something trance-like about turning pages or actively searching for your vision. I make a mental note when my heart races, my gut drops, or my head tilts sideways like a curious puppy dog. These images become rooted in my subconscious.

As I continue about my day or go for a nice drive, I look for ways I can touch, experience, borrow, or rent the images or experiences that I took note of.

As you begin to form your vision, test drive the car of your dreams, attend an open house, or take a tour of the company you are interested in. Taste their wine, drive their car, consume their product. Each activity is an opportunity to taste your vision. Take the brochure, business card, or napkin with the logo to save for your vision board.

Hopefully that consumption or experience left a lasting impression on you. Take all the images you collected. If you need more, go to the grocery store and ask for last month's magazines to buy for more resources to tear out and cut up. You can even piece together your own phrases that resonate with you.

Your clippings should evoke a feeling and have emotional power. Organize the clippings into three piles: your favorites that absolutely must be on your board, the images that you love, and another pile to save for later, just in case you want to do another vision board.

I usually grab a piece of foam board from the dollar store and start placing the images from the Favorites pile. I arrange and re-arrange the clipping into a layout that speaks to me. After my main pieces are placed on the board, I look for gaps or determine if a theme develops among the mosaic of images, trying to tie them all together like a great, intentional mural. I scour my other piles for integration and add any image that jumps out at me.

And then, the magic happens. I take a mental picture of my board, and I put all the images that I laid out back into the Favorites pile, leaving behind a blank, white, foam board. I go to sleep, letting my subconscious go to work, arranging, re-arranging, or planting new ideas into my vision.

I leave my subconscious to digest my vision and turn it into energy. Within nine days, I commit and take the glue stick and permanently affix the pictures that fulfill my vision to that foamboard.

Finally, I cut out the month and year from a magazine cover and paste it on my vision board as a final seal. Then, I place the board where it is visible every day.

Creating a vision board is a way to make your subconscious work for you. You might not have time for 100 thank-yous, 40 minutes of skill training, or being present for your family every day.

Your subconscious can do the work without you even thinking about it. Whether you include images of more money, a successful business, fancy cars, dream homes, or better relationships on your vision board, I promise that the universe, God, or the Force is working on a level that neither you nor I can see.

Have a little faith and hope. Visualization strengthens your belief in yourself, the universe, and a higher power. A vision board will make it easier on you and allow the universe to do more of the work that needs to be done. Trust me, it can handle it!

3-PEAR CHALLENGES

My parents have been married over 45 years and going, and the same and more is true for my wife's parents. Combined, they represent 100 years of parenting and marriage wisdom. I have been very fortunate to have their example for my own vision, so close to home.

As I grow my own family, I stand on the shoulders of my parent's greatness and build upon their blueprint. They allow me to design a vision for the future of our family. Perhaps you too belong to a great lineage of engineers who implanted resilient familial structures. But if you came from a family that was broken or endured divorce or abuse, use your past as fuel to propel your family and change your own children's future.

The vision board exercise reveals hidden desires and dreams, renewing energy that will help you get your groove back by reconnecting you with what matters most in your life through a fun, yet powerful process.

CHALLENGE #1 - Share Your Vision

Create your own vision board. Cut out magazine clippings and place them on the board. I recommend doing this exercise on the dining room table or in an open space where others family members can see.

For my dads who are the strong, silent type and aren't big talkers, this exercise will reveal your hopes, desires and intentions for you and your family, without ever saying or sharing a single word.

CHALLENGE #2 - Talk About Your Dreams

Tell your partner or kids about the dream you have. This will make it more real. Ask for help from people who have similar goals as you do and use them as inspiration. Spend more time with them and follow their footsteps to achieve your goal.

We are the average of the five people we spend the most time with. - Jim Rohn

CHALLENGE #3 - Sharing the Calendar

Schedule a minimum of 40 minutes every day (except Sunday) for a month to pursue your dream or goal. This daily practice will connect you with the passion and joy that your dream can provide.

Test drive the dream car, spend an hour studying marketing, build that prototype, or even practice trading or new investing strategies.

And Dads, here is a pro tip: share your calendar with your partner and family. It communicates to them what you are up to and your intentions. If they see a block of time with their name on it, they know you are committed to investing in them. They too can help you on your journey to achieve your goal.

3-PAIR TAKEAWAYS

The Adult

The time has come for your children to find their wings and fly. They will be independent in no time, setting out on their own path. But before they take flight into the world, there are still some experiences that they need from you; wisdom that only a parent can offer them.

It's not too late for those talks about sex, drugs, career, insurance, investments, and family. Now is the perfect time to share with them while it seems like your insight might finally sink in!

Make sure they have plans, with your guidance if they want, so that when life hits hard, as it inevitably will, your child won't feel lost without someone to come to for wisdom.

The Engineer

There are many ways you can design your life for success, and each day offers an opportunity to make progress. Your vision for your life is an incredible thing. You have the power to design your life as you see fit, and that makes it a true joy.

To get started, here's a quick list of three things that will help you build up your life to live your dreams today:

1. Designate time in your schedule so that it's not taken up by mindless activities. Use 40 minutes per day just for investing in yourself.

2. Every day brings new opportunities to take one or two small steps toward designing your life for success.

3. Spend some time with someone who makes you happy and you admire. Surround yourself with people who build you up.

Test this vision practice in your own life and share the fruits and success with your family. Pass on the acquired skillset of visualization that is used by master builders and CEOs.

The Adult and The Engineer

The engineer's main job is to make sure that the building lasts a long time and that it is safe to live in. Give your children blueprints, guidelines, and a code to follow so they can achieve their own dreams. Not just a beautiful building but also keys to your kingdom with your family's legacy hung above the front door.

PART III - MATURITY STAGES

As I reluctantly start to mature, I am reminded of a quote that I learnt in college from a great teacher and mentor Steve Musson. "I hope the children you once were, is proud of the adult you have now become"

With awe and wonder in my children's eyes, I know that to be true.

Chapter 8 - The Mid-Life and The Master

As we move into the middle stages of life, our days can seem mundane and repetitive. But this is an important stage in which consistency and compound returns happen. We need to be reminded of our goal, so we can master all aspects of our health and wealth.

Investing is one of the best ways to maintain focus and become masterful at what you do. Consistency and discipline in the investing world can lead to huge rewards over time. But investing is a mastery of emotions, strategy, awareness, discipline, and delayed gratification.

Can you put off the immediate rewards or gains to win in the end? I often remind myself of the Tortoise and the Hare fable. The story ends with the Tortoise who wins by being consistent and persistent.

But what you might not be aware of is how this fable also teaches a lesson in investing. It reinforces how we need to invest slowly over time and consistently sustain our investment strategy to win. This practice takes patience, but through discipline, it can lead to huge rewards later when compound interest kicks in.

There are no shortcuts or quick fixes, only a long view and the steady pace that can lead to success. Be the tortoise for your immediate family and the extended one too. Run your own race and go at your own pace.

The dedication and direction towards your own mastery will be an inspiration to those around you, even to your own children, and perhaps grandchildren at this stage in your life. Keep your mind sharp and your body strong, so you can be the best dad and granddad. Focus on living a long time so you can enjoy all of those moments spent with your family.

No one is the perfect dad, and we may never get it right. Parenting is as much about mistakes, patience, and discipline as it is about love. It's never too late for any father or mother to start investing in their family relationships, fixing any mistakes they made along the way.

Many masters travel up to a mountain alone to mediate upon life's great mysteries. But often they come back from this journey only to discover that it is the inner work that they need to focus on. That is where the true wisdom lies.

You must find peace within yourself, your family, and in this life before it can fully come together to make a difference. You must be whole, complete, and reconciled within yourself. That also means you must find peace with how you parented or raised your children.

As we look back and reflect on our parenting adventure, maybe it is time to revisit any gaps, holes, or mistakes that need to be fixed to help us feel whole and complete.

It is never too late to change your parenting style and your relationship with your children. It doesn't have to take a lifetime of parental mistakes or our children's pain as they raise their own families. We can do better by them if we just find the courage together to heal. We must learn to practice that safe space, even at this stage.

You can also fix any wrongs or hurt you've done so your family feels safe around you again. If your children seem distant from you because they think they know everything, be vulnerable and find inner peace with yourself and your family before trying to engage with them again.

No one ever said parenting was easy or just about love alone. Patience is also something we need to build time for into our lives as we get older and grow together as a family.

The truth is, as parents, we all have our individual lives and responsibilities that sometimes make it hard to stay connected with the people we love most in this world. But there are ways to master yourself and still value wisdom and unconditional love. An important takeaway is how you stay connected and engaged in the lives of your children. This is not always easy, especially if they live far away or don't want contact. It's one thing to be there when they need help, but it can also be very helpful for them to know you care about them on other days too.

More love and more care.

Am I Living my Parent's Dreams?

Everyone wants to be a master in their life. They want to have great jobs, be the best parents they can be, or become experts in their field. But what about those who are middle-aged, the ones who already have a family and are just barely making ends meet while raising kids and working full-time? Maybe they are worried about their aging parents or dealing with loss or death.

Middle-aged parents are often faced with the balancing act of raising their children and caring for aging parents. They must learn to manage being sandwiched between the stress and responsibilities of two generations, the young and old.

The answer is mastery. We must master the business of family. Not just the family business but how your family operates. The older generation can help take care of the younger generation. And the younger generation can breathe life into the older ones. The middle-aged ones can facilitate and encourage this growth, providing opportunities for this generational transfer of care, love, and resources.

I'll never master the family dynamics across three generations. But I can tell you that if you invest some time and create relationships, you can combine and leverage all the generations' love, time, and money. New babies and children always bring more love and life into a family. As a mid-career professional, you are usually the one making Chief Financial Officer decisions for your family organization. And the aging generation of grandparents are usually blessed with plenty of time. There are so many opportunities for the expression and language of love to be exchanged.

Most think of mastery as an end result, but true mastery is a way of approaching every moment with intentionality and thoughtfulness so you can create your best version of yourself and your family.

Mastery happens when you're fully engaged in a venture that inspires and excites you on a deep level and your whole life comes together around it. The quest for mastery is never-ending. It starts with self-love and acceptance of where we are now. Then, we move on to try new pursuits and eventually become masters at them too.

Today, many people live longer and healthier lives than ever before. Leveraging that time gives us an incredible opportunity to grow and learn new skills that we can then share with our children and grandchildren.

One key area where this mastery learning process needs attention is in the areas of investment, life, and family coaching. Managing your finances well, getting clarity on what you want out of life, and honing our parenting methods, these are all skills that take focused practice to master.

There are many people who put in the time to achieve mastery. They continually practice well above the suggested 40 minutes a day to reach their goals. Whether it be working out, cooking, reading, coding, or even spending time with your children, we should all carve out time dedicated to what is truly important.

For me, that focus was my health. For many years, while in the pursuit of happiness, money, and ambition, I neglected and de-prioritized my health. I learned that lifestyle from my overweight, aging, diabetic, parents. I watched them struggle with their health while they provided food on the table, a roof over my head, and activities to grow my skills and value in society. And I played their game, living by the script that they wrote, dreamt, and created for me. I subscribed to this lifestyle unconsciously; it was my inception. I thought it was mine, so I became a successful public servant, doing government work, climbing the corporate ladder. I walked the same path as my mom at first but left that career to fulfill my dad's passion for making films and shows for a major production company.

It wasn't until I spent years on dual careers that I realized my parents' dreams were not my own. I spent ten years living the life my mom wanted me to live. Ten years, trying to fulfill her career dreams in finance and public service. And I spent another 20 years chasing my father's passion for film and television, both behind and in front of the camera.

I continued working at their dreams until the pandemic, when I was forced to shut it down. Suddenly, I was placed in isolation from my constant thriving and hustling. The pandemic stopped everything that was non-essential. As our leaders valued human life above all else, the government dictating what was important and essential.

In all honesty, I needed a forced lockdown to discover and identify my own expectations, dreams, hopes, and desires. You are not your parents, nor are you society or the unspoken expectations or norms of those around you. You must become who you are. How you shape that self, consciously and sub-consciously, that part is up to you.

3-PARE CHALLENGES

After realizing that I modeled a life based on my mom's dreams and ambitions with government service, I felt even more lost, confused, and desperate to find my true path. I hit my head against the glass ceiling at the same time my online-retail company was pivoting and there were massive changes in the market. I questioned my purpose and who I was as a person. I no longer was sure of what was I chasing. What was I trying to accomplish with my life?

It took me until my late 30s to have the courage to search and find a passion of my own to master and focus on in my life. But this choice helped me become happier than I had felt in years. For me, that mastery focused on investing and coaching. My investing practice was a gift that I never expected would bring me so much of my own freedom, including the opportunity to write this book and share tips to create a brighter future for you too.

Before I could set sail my own adventure, my own path, I had to lose some baggage that I carried with me. The emotional baggage included my parent's dreams of who I should be, the feelings I wore on my waistline, and the rat race I joined in, looking for the cheese. And bacon, as well.

I am still dropping off extra weight, eliminating stressors, distancing from toxic people, and clearing my plate so it isn't as full or heavy. These challenges will help you do the same, cutting out the habits that don't serve you, and poison your purpose.

CHALLENGE #1 - Portion Control

Cut down your food portions. The movie, *Super Size Me,* showed us the problems with junk food, but in North America, the food industry has stretched our stomachs with larger portions, and less nutrient-dense foods. As we eat larger quantities, we also have to eat more frequently because we aren't getting quality nutrition.

My fitness and nutrition coach taught me this technique for how to control your portions, which is perfectly matched to you, specifically.

The bigger the hand, the larger the portion.

- Palm of Protein
- Fistful of Veggies
- Handful of Carbs
- Thumb of Fat

CHALLENGE #2 - Get Cut for Weigh-In

Get a digital scale that has several different fitness metrics such as weight, body fat percentage, subcutaneous fat, body mass index, bone mass, body water, muscle masses, etc. Pick the metric you want to target and work on it. For me, I focused on my body fat percentage instead of a specific weight which is a better match for me and my goals.

Regardless of the measure you choose, tracking your body metrics will tell you how fit you are. And your performance can only improve if you can measure where you are at and how far you've come. The scale doesn't lie.

CHALLENGE #3 - Say Goodbye to Excess

The other challenges have focused on the physical, but this one is based in the realm of emotions and energy. Cut out extracurricular activities that don't promote life or energy. This paring challenge may include friends, coworkers or even some relatives. Life is too short to give someone your time who isn't there to build you up. Don't let energy leeches bleed you dry or drag you down. Misery loves company, so it is time to say goodbye and to make way for something new and life-giving.

Dad Bods and Father Figures

I was typical yo-yo dad. I had my ups and downs with my family relationships, work-life balance, and stress levels. But then I had a wake-up call that caused me to question the way I lived my life.

It might have something to do with that really "rough week," which catapulted me into an early mid-life crisis and caused me to shift my focus onto me.

I was sick and tired of making everyone else happy, making a better life for them. Every decision I made was for someone else. I finally realized how empty, insecure, and broken I was. That discovery led me on a new journey of transformation. I came to the understanding that if I didn't make some changes in my life, then I would be headed for an early grave.

And here, in this place of desperation and decision, is where the mundane meets variety.

Many of us struggle when we reach the end of a mastery cycle for our common dreams. Maybe we have to face the realization that we have not dared or dreamt enough. Some reach a level of comfort and contentment, but even those will come to a period in their middle years when their soul craves a little variety, a spark, or an introduction to something new.

Typical images from my pre-loaded mid-life catalog invoked a shiny, red, two-door sports car with at least 350 horses under the hood. But even after I bought my new toys and gadgets, I knew I needed something other than material things. I needed a physical and mental change in myself. If I was so broken, I had to build my esteem, my belief in self, not in my abilities, but in my worth. Not just my net worth from investing but knowing that I am worthy. Worthy of love, worthy of time, and worthy of self-care without conditions or work. Just plain me, as is. Worthy.

We need to grow a new image of middle age. A friend and coach once told me, that instead of the accepting the classic Dad Bod, we could create new Father Figure bodies that are healthy, strong, and fit. Coach "Chappy" is a cancer survivor, a father of two, and a beam of light for many communities. As a local hero, he continues to reach others through the amazing organizations he supports.

Coach Chapmann is probably 15 years my senior, but he can still beat me in a volleyball match, a run, or a fitness challenge. His circle is filled with elite and professional athletes. Being surrounded by the best spills over to affect his life in a positive way.

I took my youth and the boundless energy from that stage for granted. As I grew older, I did not keep up with the friends or the fitness that I performed when I was younger. I prioritized my wife's needs and those of my daughters after that. You might not have a chance to work out or train with professional athletes but find your own community of support. I found a fitness community with younger and older generations working out together which is so inspiring. This group was introduced to me via some members in my faith community.

Keep adding to your network and continue to surround yourself with inspiring people, even if you can only meet digitally right now. Good people know other good and great people.

3-PEAR CHALLENGES

A great father figure is someone who listens to your ideas and then helps you find a way to make them happen. He is there for you when circumstances are going well, but also when they're not. A great dad encourages his kids in every pursuit, whether it's playing sports or pursuing a career.

It doesn't matter what career path you choose to take in life, whether a stay-at-home dad or a corporate CEO. What counts is that you are there for your family and give them the love and support they need through tough times.

Those lessons, those memories, will last longer and be more valuable than any dollar amount that you choose to leave behind.

You need to be around to make more of those memories. Remember, this is just the middle of your life, and you have plenty of life to live. So, these challenges are designed to promote your health and longevity.

CHALLENGE #1 - Drink Water

Aim to drink about three liters of water per day. Become the master of drinking water, which is a key to regulating our body's temperature, hormones, digestion, blood viscosity, brain cushion, and waste processing in our body.

Dads, you wouldn't run your car on an empty tank or drive it on fumes. So, fuel up and drink your water. A full tank, please.

CHALLENGE #2 - Wellness Coaching

Find a person who can help you with your health. They might be a fitness coach, nutritionist, or someone for your mindset. If you are like me, you may have ignored your own health while taking care of other people. But to provide better care for the people you love, it is important to take care of yourself first.

CHALLENGE #3 - Community and Accountability

Build a community of support and accountability. Join an existing hobby or interest group, start a new class, and do it together with a family member or friend. As we get older, our networks tend to shrink, and our groups tighten. Very rarely do our circles of influence grow. So, find a peer that is on the same journey as you and travel together towards health. See what fruits may grow from this new mastery and partnership of accountability. Networking with others helps us to realize that we are not alone in our journey. We are better together on the road to improvement and mastery.

3-PAIR TAKEAWAYS

The Middle Age

If you're in the middle of your life, then you are sandwiched between a younger generation and an older one. We often forget that there is a master plan for our lives. If you think about your life as one big story, then you can start living with purpose.

This age is a time for deep and prolonged work. Be sure to remember what you want your story to be. The best way to grow is by investing in yourself. That means taking risks, listening to your gut feeling, and following your own dreams.

The Master

What does it take to be the master of your domain? You must develop the ability to stay on the path, even when faced with obstacles. Is your goal in life to have peace and happiness? There are many routes that will lead you there, but the one element they all have in common is staying focused on reaching your goal, no matter what stands in your way.

A master has a healthy mindset and is committed to achieving his goals. He understands what those goals should be and how to prioritize them, in order to stay on his chosen path. With this knowledge, he can make decisions quickly about when or if an endeavor is worth doing. With these skills in place, there's no telling where he'll end up!

The Middle Age and The Master

The relationship between a master and an adult learner is one of the most beautiful connections in life. When someone seeks out a mentor, they are looking for wisdom that will help them achieve their goals.

When this relationship still happens at this stage between parent and child, it is true gift. It must mean there is much to learn from the master, and the student continues to grow.

While some people might think one can only take from the master, both sides must be willing to give to create that true connection. If you have achieved success, I encourage you to give back by mentoring and guiding those who need it. The path that the master is on is a worthy and fruitful one. No one wants to be on the narrow path of success alone.

Chapter 9 - The Retiree and The Legend

Most people think of their golden years as a time for relaxing, enjoying hobbies, and traveling. But what if these activities don't provide the sense of fulfillment that's been missing in your life? What would you do then?

What does retirement mean to you?

Retirement is not the end-all be-all; it's just another chapter in your life. It also doesn't have to be a financial burden. Whether you retire early or later on in life, knowing how to live mindfully can help you find more meaning than ever before.

What do you want to be when you grow older? And what will you do with fewer responsibilities and more time in your life?

I enjoy the privilege of seeing my parents in their retirement years. They provide me with priceless insight and wisdom on what it means to retire at a young age. I've been blessed to watch them navigate their new lives with grace and sharp wit.

What is most fascinating for me is how they spend their time since retiring. They read the newspaper, garden, socialize at the clubhouse, cook new dishes and cuisine, take quarterly vacations and cruises, go to more church services, do chair exercises, and watch lots of daytime dramas and soap operas, which is a true sign of retirement.

I learned a lot about the value of financial independence and enjoyment in the golden years. Yet it saddens me that my children will never know them as working adults.

Their view of their grandparents will be very different than my memory of my parents growing up. My kids see them in this golden time of harvest. Yet, my memory of my parents was of lean spending and long work hours, trading time for a pension. I got to see my parents struggle, fight, and climb to success. Their work ethic also fuels some of my own drives.

Retirement is a chance to use your time to be a living legend. Live out your dream, experience that little slice of heaven on Earth. That is why they call these years the golden ones. Hopefully, you created your Golden Goose and are reaping the rewards of its golden eggs. So many of my investing peers are in this stage, living on a farm or by a lake, spending their time at ski resorts or racing cars, living their best lives.

My mentor Phil Town and his daughter Danielle Town have a wonderful relationship. Phil is an old Vietnam ex-Green Beret and a member of the Special Forces. It took decades before his daughter, a successful venture capitalist lawyer, turned to her own dad for investing advice. I hope it doesn't take that long for my daughters to learn from me the importance of taking care of the golden goose and the cash cow too!

I am just beginning to change my family's financial future forever. By investing my own money, as well as my family's, I give them a chance to retire comfortably. I was always concerned and worried about if my parents had enough to survive on because my mom had a pension, but my dad did not.

A person who is about to retire may have some math they need to think about. We typically work for 40 years, saving money while we work so that we can live off of the money for another 40 years when we retire. Most of us can save enough money while working to afford the future. But the math doesn't work if you don't invest your money. Many older people must keep working because they didn't save enough money, or they spend too much on living costs during retirement.

Investing is CRITICAL for everyone to learn so they don't have to work through retirement. And I'm sorry to say that setting aside money for the future isn't a priority for most people. Too often they adopt habits of fulfilling immediate wants, like ordering from Amazon or loading movies on demand from Netflix within a minute of deciding what they want. Retirement and investing don't work like that; you cannot order or load your investments instantaneously. Your savings must be grown and cultivated over time, while simultaneously working and earning that money.

This practice of long-term savings is worth investing in. It is the only way retirement works, and I want you to retire. You shouldn't have to work until you are 70 or 80 because your expenses are too high, or you don't have enough saved to cover your monthly bills.

I want you to be that legendary example of a retiree, one who is financially free, with an abundance of time, fit and healthier than when you were in your working years. I encourage to learn how to both invest for yourself and in yourself. Be that Legend.

Funding and Finding the Golden Expedition

As I approach my retirement years, I am learning how to live the life of a legend, along with my parents. I financially free, have an abundance of time, and am healthier than in my stressful working years. The best part is, I am not even 45-years old yet!

I get to do all the activities I want and need to do with my days, from traveling to playing golf or reading books in the afternoons. While some days may not be as lucrative as when I was working full-time, these bonuses are what retirement feels like for me:

- Waking up without an alarm clock.
- Making four figures before breakfast while still in my PJ's.
- Taking my daughters to school and playdates mid-week.
- Helping my church with livestreaming services.
- Hiring a personal trainer and losing 35 pounds and counting.
- Surrounding myself with gurus, good chats, and coffee.
- Cooking amazing, flavorful, and healthy meals for my family.
- Putting my kids to bed and reading them bedtime stories.
- Writing this book while my wife reads beside me.

What do you want to enjoy when you retire? Can you imagine a time in your life when you don't have the mental stress of a demanding job? Or having the security to know that all the monthly bills are paid for decades to come? Perhaps you can visit your family and friends anytime, anywhere in the world, at least once all the travel restrictions are lifted after the pandemic.

Retirement will look different for each person, but now is the time to step into that Legendary idea or become the person you always wanted to be. Retirement is the time to be honest so you can re-orient yourself and find a purpose that will continually fill you up.

The more truthful you can be with your thoughts and actions, the easier life becomes. When we're true to ourselves, we attract those items, experiences, and people into our lives that make us happy. The quest to obtain these experiences, items, and people to join you is what I refer to as, "Finding your Golden Expedition."

The tendency is for most retirees is to just coast through their days in retirement, get by, or live with scarcity because they are worried about draining their retirement account. My recommendation is for you to reach out to someone you trust who can help you with your nest egg. Find someone who can teach you how to manage and keep your golden goose healthy.

For those who think they are too old to start investing, remember that Warren Buffett is 90 years old, and his investing partner Charlie Munger is 97 years old. They both actively invested well into their golden years to fund their own adventures.

Retirement offers so many opportunities for exploration, though there may be challenges to overcome if you don't prepare properly beforehand. It's important to consider investing before retiring to make sure your retirement years are truly golden.

3-PARE CHALLENGES

In retirement, many people have to cut back on their budgets. One way to pare your spending is to is to cut out cable TV subscriptions or morning coffee from a coffee shop. These expenses can add up quickly and make it hard to pay for them all.

A recipe for a healthy financial balance has always been to spend less than you earn. However, when you enter the retirement phase, you should change your motto to, "Spend less than you have budgeted." This idea assumes you have enough resources to live off of for a few decades.

When you retire, you will not have to work every day. But you will cut out your commute in rush hour, cut down the mental stresses and pressure of performing, and ultimately cut away eight hours of tasks from your day.

Just because you are not working, doesn't mean that you can't earn an income. Again, investing is the answer to keeping your financial golden goose alive versus cooking it. It allows you to crack open your nest egg and eat your retirement omelette. As the CFO of your family, you choose which mentality or strategy to follow, one of lack or one of abundance.

But being retired is not all fun and games. It is important to plan for your new life. I encourage you, no matter what retirement situation you are in, to cut your expenses and invest your money.

While you focus on cutting worries, doubts, and concerns from your life, I also encourage you to look, not at just your financial burdens, but also at what emotional baggage you need to let go of. Cut and eliminate any regrets you may be holding on to.

Here are some challenges that will help with cutting out financial and emotional burdens.

CHALLENGE #1 - Senior Discounts

A fun way to save money and cut down your expenses for retirees is to look for discounts or coupons for seniors (55+). Look at your expenses from grocery stores, drug stores, travel, and financial institutions. Some of the benefits are:

- 10-15% discount on a regular basis.
- 20-30% discounts on specific days.
- 30-45% rebates on household upgrades.
- Free complementary drinks with meal.
- Free passes and tickets for transportation.
- Free bank chequing and savings accounts.

Look at your itemized receipts and statements to find how you can get items at a discounted rate or for free. Saving 10-45% from your regular expenses could fund your golden expedition. Have fun cutting out coupons!

CHALLENGE #2 - Cut out the Middleman

As a retiree, your fiduciary responsibility to your children and work are considerably less. Shift your attention and caring to your retirement investments. Many funds and accounts that you hold or invest in are managed by an advisor or portfolio manager who charges you a fee for passive management.

Why would you trust and pay a management fee to someone who isn't vested in your returns? Their payment isn't based on their performance or their active management. Typical management fees range from 1-2% of your portfolio account per year.

With a bit of time, focus, and knowledge, you can become a better investor than your current advisor or portfolio manager. You can do it yourself, keep a better eye on your financial earnings, invest better, and save on the fees.

CHALLENGE #3 - Cut the Regrets

This is the hardest challenge of all and might take the most time. It's a good thing that you are retired and have an abundance of this resources to use.

Healing old wounds takes time. Leave your regrets behind and lighten your load for the final leg of your golden journey. Focus on healing your relationships that, in turn, will increase your overall wealth.

These six statements can identify and help with letting go of regret.

1. Name your regret. "I feel guilty because…"
2. Make amends. "I'm sorry for…"
3. Learn from mistakes. "I have since learned that…"
4. Find compassion. "I take responsibility for…"
5. Embrace gratitude. "I am thankful that…"
6. Share and support. "What I am working on is…"

Working through regret and letting go is a complex and complicated process. Completing these six statements will hopefully prompt you in your recovery. Learn to let go of your guilt and regret which can affect relationships and add mental and physical stress.

Regrets belong in the past. Make your peace with your past and keep it where it belongs.

May the Force Be with You. And Also with You.

If you've ever been in a situation where your back is up against the wall and there was no way out, then you know how it feels to be suffocating or stuck. Whatever your stress or problem is like, we may feel like the world is coming to an end and that we are on our own.

This stuck and rigid mentality is a mind trap that many retirees can fall into. During the global pandemic, we lived in an unprecedented time which made the future more uncertain concerning jobs, food, fuel, and investments.

It can be hard to deal with all of the pressures in your life. All you want is an escape route, but you keep holding it all in. Cracks form, and your foundation starts to crumble. What do you do when life doesn't go according to plan? How do you react when your investments are down, your relationships are broken, and the world seems dark, corrupt, and hopeless?

There's a concept called "faith" that helps people who are going through tough times. Faith reminds you that there are things you can't control, and those circumstances are up to a higher power. It is this faith that reminds people to be thankful for what they have because it isn't owed to them.

For some people, God is their higher power. Others might see the higher power as a spiritual light or a feeling of alignment with the universe. Most kids today know it as the "Force" thanks to Star Wars and Disney. When you talk to this spirit or power, you can trust it more as you become more in tune with it.

If you have a strong connection with this power, you can ride on it and use its waves to do things for yourself. You may be able to harvest fruit from its waves or bathe in blessings if they come your way.

The Force operates on a different plane, the spiritual one. We can't see, touch, or fully explain this force, but with time and training, we can feel it. It is the same spirit that helps transform two cells into a newborn baby, the same plane where your love and your bond for your family exists. It also helps plants grow and the oceans move.

The Force is inside of us, and it cannot be fully understood or controlled. But that does not mean we should not use it or connect to that force. We can use its power to our advantage. Even if we do not know how it works, we can still use it to help us.

Like the computer, most of us don't understand fully how it functions. We aren't programmers nor do we understand circuits, processors, or microchips. But we can still use our computers to do basic tasks like send an email or type a document. Just like a connected computer functions to make life easier, this Force was also designed to help you.

Yes, belief or faith takes learning, patience, and requires some time to get to know it. But faith is another aspect of life that is worth your investment, because if you master this spiritual force and power called Faith, it will make parenting, investing, and life so much easier. You'll work with the universe and its flow rather than against it.

So much of this book is dedicated to the mind and the body, from attitude and perspective adjustments to physical challenges and bio-hacks. Yet, I would do you a disservice if I didn't mention the spiritual forces and how you can align yourself with the universe.

As we move towards the end of this book and the end of the human life development, we must consider life after death. Some might wonder about what happens to them after they die. It is my belief that we get reunited or go back to that source, that my soul lives on, and my spiritual body goes to be with my God. To me that is a comfort.

Other might think about the people they leave behind. It is not too late to do something for those you leave behind, to reinforce your efforts and reap the fruits of your labour. Retirement is a time to be a living legend for those people. You may feel that leaving a golden goose and financial estate behind is a way to become a legend. But I've identified something more valuable and precious than your money. It is the moments and memories you leave behind.

- Special skills you teach.
- Values you instill.
- Favorite recipes you share.
- Holiday traditions you keep.
- Family vacations you take.

3-PEAR CHALLENGES

One of the best things you can do with all the retirement time in your life is to spend it with your kids and grandkids. You will have a lot of fun and feel less stressed.

If you live further away from your family or are not into community living, you might want to fulfill that need for companionship with a furry friend. For many golden year individuals, a pet or another source of love can bring a sense of purpose with daily feedings, care giving, and more physically activity. Daily walks with your pet can combat a sedentary lifestyle, instead of sitting and watching the news or afternoon soap operas.

Retirement is a good time to do what you want because you have more time. You can learn new skills, have fun, and try new activities, like doing volunteer work. Retirees can help by giving money or volunteering their time to make the world better.

And there are many experiences left to enjoy. So, seek to connect to your family, society, and your community because they could benefit from your participation and presence.

The following challenges are designed to help move and inspire the retiree to become a legend within their circle of influence, their own families, and even with their young, old, and furry friends.

CHALLENGE #1 - Make More Memories

Plan family activities that can create wonderful memories. Those remembrances are the only items that you can take with you for your next life-stage journey. So, fill your monthly calendar with at least one event you can capture with a photo to fill up an album or hang on your fridge.

As you plan, remember the five ways you can show your love and make an impact with your family. Send an encouraging letter in the mail, be of service by taking care of your grandchildren once a week, or try something bigger, like spending a holiday getaway at a resort or celebrating at a formal dining establishment together. Be the legend and make it memorable.

"For the Gram" is a slang term that young people use, meaning to capture a picture to post on Instagram. But I think this can be adopted by Grandmas as well, to capture special memories to post on their walls.

CHALLENGE #2 - Create New Companionships

Foster a dog for a week. See how it feels to care for man's best friend. Determine if there is a match in energy, personality, and companionship. Take two walks a day with your new furry friend, rain or shine.

Pick a charity or organization and figure out how you can contribute to their operations. You may choose a soup kitchen, your local church, or even at a nearby hospital, just providing company to those who are alone.

The true riches in life are in the connections we create. These connections are an important part to living a fulfilled and wealthy life.

CHALLENGE #3 - Your Final Wishes.

If you are a parent planning to leave your next generation or grandchildren with an inheritance, think about how you could gift that inheritance while you are still here to make sure it goes how you planned. Consider putting properties in your children's names or setting up tax-efficient companies to handle your assets.

Wealth transfers and final expenses are often areas that are not thought about or discussed openly or honestly. Our final wishes can have a morbid connotation, and families tend to shy away from talking about them.

But, if you have your inheritance planned out, and you know your intentions, share them so you can plan a successful and tax-efficient transfer of assets. This talk can also initiate guidelines or structure for your heirs to follow while they are grieving. These conversations can be the start of your Will.

3-PAIR TAKEAWAYS

The Retired

The truth is that there is no clear answer for what retirement means or looks like. It can also be hard for you to find your place in the world after working for so long.

After retirement, you might feel bored or lonely. You may also feel like a burden to others. You don't need to feel this way! You can still have a good time when you retire by changing your mindset and finding your "why."

Your "why" will probably change after you retire, but it's important to enjoy yourself and get back that youthful energy!

The Legend

Be a legend to your family, friends, and community. What do you want to be remembered for? This is the stage in life to take the actions that will live on for generations.

So, make some memories with your family and friends. This can look like family traditions, weekend getaways, or celebrations at a formal restaurant or venue. Commemorate these events and memories with photos that capture the moments. Create as many memories as you can and fill up your photo album or wall with pictures from your creations.

The Retired and The Legend

Your family needs to know what you want to happen after you pass on. Having tough conversations concerning your final wishes, expectations, and the division and transfer of assets is important. You don't want your children to fight over your possessions, especially if you aren't open and clear with them about your intentions.

The best way to make a smooth transfer is to complete it while you are still here, not during a time of grieving. These conversations can set expectation and even create opportunities to make a more efficient wealth transfer. This discussion is a great start to creating an official will.

Be a living legend and enjoy seeing the benefits and the fruit of your efforts today, instead of leaving it all behind.

Chapter 10 - The Transcended and The Legacy

When I hear the word legacy, I think of those great leaders who have passed on. Martin Luther King, Jr., an activist who led with non-violence and shared his famous dream regarding civil rights. Or Mother Teresa, a Catholic nun who spent her life caring for lepers, the homeless, and the dying.

Not all legacies are famously known to whole world. But there are legacies closer to home that can make a world difference in the lives of others. I had the privilege of being a part of my Auntie Mimie Ho's legacy. Her legacy was as a dedicated teacher who promoted Chinese culture through language and traditional dance.

She spent 35 years teaching Chinese (Mandarin) in the public education system. During the evenings and weekends, she taught Chinese dance to multiple generations. Several times per year, her dancers and dance company were invited to perform on international stages and at festivals all over the world.

Several years ago, I was roped in to be one of her many young teenage performers. Now, as a middle-aged man, I still march in the Chinese New Year parades to honor her legacy. Over 10,000 people come every year to celebrate her legacy and to watch the students of her students dance.

Some of those students started a foundation in her name to carry on her work and legacy. The Maria Mimie Ho Foundation's aims are to:

- Promote and preserve Chinese culture through dance and language.
- Provide opportunities for youth to experience and appreciate cultural diversity.
- Bridge cultural gaps through teaching and education.
- Help youth realize their dreams to succeed in life.

https://www.mmhofoundation.org/mission/

It has been over 10 years since Mimie passed, and even though she isn't there to teach her classes anymore, students still receive grants and scholarships to develop their Mandarin language skills. Her traditional Chinese dance company is run by a former student who still teaches classes on the weekends. The studio also conducts workshops and performances for people of all ages via her foundation.

Auntie Mimie's vehicle for her legacy was definitely dance, but people remember her and honor her because of the beliefs she held. She loved youth and understood the importance of teaching them, not just dance skills, but life skills.

Legacy is a word that can be defined in many ways. It is often used to describe the lasting achievements of someone's life, or the effects one person has on future generations.

Even an act of kindness from a stranger may leave such a positive impression on you that it inspires you to help others in your community. This compassion can have a ripple effect for years to come.

A legacy has two important elements:

1. Tangible objects like schools, hospitals, parks, or monuments, as well as foundations, scholarships, and funds.

2. Intangible items like sharing knowledge with younger generations through mentoring, coaching, or teaching values and ethics.

We all have an obligation to make the world a better place for future generations. This responsibility is even greater when it comes to our families and our communities. It's easy to focus on what will happen after you die, but your legacy can be about more than just money or material goods. Like the great leaders mentioned above, we want to embed our value and ethics in our legacies.

Prostate and Probate: Both are Bad for Dads

Inevitably, at some point in life, you're going to have to go through a prostate exam. It's not just any old examination though. This type of exam can be one of the most uncomfortable experiences that ever happens to you.

The doctor will stick his finger up your butt and then he'll push on your bladder until it hurts. Your prostate is located near your urethra, so the doctor will also feel around for lumps or anything else that might be wrong with your "P-spot."

Your chances of being diagnosed with prostate issues are 50%. One out of every seven men will develop prostate cancer, a deadly issue. So, chances that you will encounter or be affected by prostate concerns are quite high and unavoidable.

Probate, however, is not a medical condition. It is commonly referred to as a death tax or estate fee. Often, whatever you saved up or intended to go to your family as an inheritance will be eaten up by court fees. Probate even occurs if you have a clear, dated, and signed will or beneficiaries assigned. Probate is something that will happen 100% of the time unless you do something to better manage your estate.

If your wishes were to leave your house, pension, or investment portfolio to your kids or grandchildren without a plan to transfer them, the courts (probate) will decide how your inheritance is distributed for you. If your estate or capital gains are quite substantial, it is possible to for your kin to receive only a mere fraction of what you expected to pass on.

There is nothing you can do or say about how the probate acts because you are gone. Your will can be contested, and the probate courts will make the final decision about how your inheritance is allocated, distributed, and taxed.

Not only can the results be damaging, but the lengthy duration of time before the courts decide can wreak havoc and add stress to a family dynamic, especially during a time of mourning. The process of probate usually takes three months minimum to verify the will, sort out titles and beneficiaries, identify assets, and pay any final taxes that are due.

Meanwhile the family executor, if one is appointed, may have to shoulder the costs and burden of the estate, until a decision is made.

Parents never get to see the effects of their lack of planning or lack of communicating clear expectations and wishes. The stress, drama, and trauma are instead felt by the kin who are left to clean up the mess which was intended as a gift.

3-PARE CHALLENGES

Final expenses are not the legacy you want to leave behind for your kids. Don't make them scramble to find your pension papers, stock investments, safety deposit keys, life insurance policy papers, or land title documents. Don't leave them paying for funeral arrangements and outstanding debts.

A financial legacy can be a gift of money or some other asset that you leave behind for your family, friends, colleagues, or community. This legacy is a culmination of money, assets, and investments, an inheritance you leave behind for your beneficiaries.

These assets usually have to pass through the hands of the court system to verify that they belonged to you, that they are directed and allocated appropriately, and that the will is not contested. There is usually a very large bill and a lengthy process associated with these typical probate services.

Most dads think, "Why should I care? They should be lucky to even get anything after I die." Well, this "gift" of probate is probably not the last experience you want to give your kids for your legacy.

So, here are some challenges to help eliminate a painful wealth transfer during a sensitive and sorrowful time for the family you left behind.

CHALLENGE #1 - Pick Your Plot

Choose your final resting place ahead of time. Save your family from drawing straws and just settling for the place to put your body. Be more intentional about your final plan. Imagine, what might happen a year after your passing. Is it easy for your family and friends to find you in the cemetery? Can you picture them as they park close by and walk to your grave, holding some flowers to have a heart-filled talk?

You can dictate and control that experience for your kin. It is never easy visiting a loved one who is long gone. Be intentional and mindful beyond the grave, continuing your legacy of care.

CHALLENGE #2 - Cut a Key

Make a copy of your house, car, and security box keys. This thoughtful act gives your trusted ones access to your:

- Property titles/ deeds
- Financial documents
- Insurance beneficiaries
- Medical contact information
- Living will and last will

These trusted people may include your executor and your medical or financial power of attorney. Remember, with new technology, do not forget to include your digital assets, social accounts, device access, and passwords.

Make copies of these important documents and store at least one set in your home and the other in a bank safety-deposit box. Typically, these boxes are discounted or receive a tax write-off for seniors.

CHALLENGE #3 - Cut to the Chase

Talking about death and your final preparations can be very morbid and triggering for most families. No one wants to think about a life without their parents or arranging the details of their death.

That emotional response is why the parent has to take charge. Just cut to the chase. There is no easy way to start, so bring your wishes up during a conversation or slip the topic into dinner talk. Here are a couple of tips on how to approach this sensitive topic.

Just cut to the chase and say to your kin, "*I need you to remember three important things, when I pass away or if I get really sick. I've prepared these for you.*"

Then show them:

1. The **keys**
2. The **physical binder/ folder** of important documents, but not the contents inside
3. The **two locations** where you keep these items

Note: You have just shared a heavily loaded message. Treat it like plutonium, safe to touch and handle if it's solid, but extremely explosive in different states or in the wrong hands.

Who is Trusteed to Fund the Party?

A trust fund is one way to protect assets for your future generations. It can also be used to provide income for you and your family members during retirement, reduce the amount of any death taxes, and bypass probate fees all together.

A family trust fund can be created by a **settlor (parent)**, who typically contributes the **assets (investments, property, business)** on behalf of the **beneficiary (children/ grandchildren).** All of these assets are managed by a **trustee (a living parent/ successor).**

This Family Trust owns the assets and makes investment decisions, which are separate from the beneficiaries' personal affairs. A trust fund can be a separate entity or person who manages the assets the fund holds. This financial tool is not just for high-net-worth clients. Everyday middle-class folks can also benefit from these estate-planning strategies involving trusts.

A trust fund can provide peace of mind, knowing that you've done everything possible to protect what matters most, your family. It is the vehicle for holding all the tangible aspects of your financial legacy. This trust entity can manage your properties, distribute dividends, and shelter your family from costly taxes and probate fees for multiple generations.

The Chinese have a proverb, "Wealth does not last beyond three generations," while Americans say, "The first generation makes the money, the second spends it, and the third loses it." It is unclear who gets to claim the rights to this concept, Confucius or Andrew Carnegie. But what these sayings make clear, whether you live in Asia or America, is that three-generation wealth trends seem to be true across the board.

So many family businesses and empires fail because of these three-generational wealth curses. You might even believe that financial legacy is now a myth, or even worse, just a forgotten memory. My theory is that the legacy fails due to a missing component, the intangible other half of the equation of the legacy creation.

The intangible part of building a legacy is how we teach, coach, and provide opportunities throughout our children's lives to learn strong values and ethics.

We must pass on the values and ethics of communicating, resiliency, compassion, planning, and awareness. The Trust you create may only last for three generations. To grow it beyond that point will take more than a financial investment. The success of your legacy will be in correlation with the amount of love, energy, and care you invest in those around you.

3-PEAR CHALLENGES

While writing this chapter and remembering the legacy of my Auntie Mimie Ho, I asked her daughter, my cousin Valerie to share with me her favorite memories of her mom related to dance.

The first memory Valerie shared was of her mom yelling. She laughed as she fondly remembered her mother's intensity. If you were really close to my aunt, and if she felt comfortable with you, you got the tough-love Asian communication style of, "Louder will make it clearer!"

Valerie's second memory was of watching her mom emcee a performance and how she talked up the dance and the dancers. You could hear the joy in Auntie Mimie's voice as she spoke of her culture. She felt such pride in showcasing these performances to the next generation as they learned about their heritage and participated in preserving it.

The third memory my cousin shared was more personal:

> *"I think I was eight, and I remember we had a show at the Bay downtown. I wasn't feeling well. Feeling really sick. I didn't want to dance. She begged me to do the show, so I sucked it up and even performed it really well. I put extra feeling into it to hide the fact I was feeling like garbage. When the show was over, she gave me a big hug and smile. Up to that point she never saw me perform that well. She was really proud.*
>
> *It was one of the few times I remember her hugging me in my childhood. And on top of it, it meant a lot because she was very difficult to impress.*
>
> *That was also an a-ha moment for me as a dancer and performer. I understood that putting character and feeling wasn't that out of reach or hard."*

These are the types of lessons and moments that I hope my kids and I will share. After you are gone, your children will remember how you supported them and how you taught them to be successful in life.

It's never too early to start teaching your kids about the importance of investing in themselves. The earlier you teach them, the more likely they will grow up with a mindset that allows them to take care of their own needs and carry on so your grandchildren, your great-grandchildren, and even your great, great-grandchildren will honor and enjoy your legacy.

The following challenges will help you develop the intangible values and ethics of your legacy while supporting it with the tangible, financial backing of a family trust.

CHALLENGE #1 - A Will and Trust

If you plan to leave your assets, investments, and property to your children, and you want to ensure that the wealth transfer is fast, efficient, and executed to your wishes, then forming a trust company may be in your family's best interest.

Research the types of family trusts in your area. Consider asking your lawyer or local pro-bono service which type of trust may be right for your situation.

CHALLENGE #2 - Foundation or Charity

Some people might have no one in their family to carry on their life's work or legacy. These people may choose to support a foundation or institution that shares their values. For example, if you care about education, support your local school system so it can continue to teach children.

Many organizations could benefit from a sizable contribution to carry on their mission. And you could be the angel investor who makes that legacy possible.

CHALLENGE #3 - Epitaph inscriptions

Most of the world may not know our name or our story. We may never have a statue erected for our work. But we can tell others our message, simply by sharing it on our own plot of land from beyond the grave.

An epitaph is a tombstone or plaque with a personal message inscribed on it. This inscription is usually a saying from the deceased person or a last word. Visit a cemetery to discover what words and wisdom others have shared.

3-PAIR TAKEAWAYS

The Transcended

When people pass, they rarely think about how they will leave their belongings. An unexpected departure can create a burden of final expenses and stresses to an already grief-stricken family.

Avoid this pitfall by mindfully preparing the necessary documents and access to your information to those you trust. Express your wishes verbally and on paper, in the form of a will. This important document lays out your final wishes and can also provide some comfort, knowing that you can shape how you are remembered.

Plan your final resting place.

The Legacy

A legacy is hard to define because it is only recognized once all the work has been done, and the person has passed.

A legacy is comprised of two parts: tangible assets and intangible family memories. The first, tangible assets, are the physical things that a person leaves behind when they die, their homes, cars, and investments.

The second part of a legacy is the intangible family memories. This part is more difficult to control because it is based on what people think about you after you're gone. These impressions include if your kids turned out well or how much happiness your life brought to those around you.

Oftentimes, people focus on only one of these components of their legacy. But if you can build both tangible and intangible assets, a family trust has a chance of providing financially and emotionally for multiple generations.

The Transcended and The Legacy

Your burial site is that place where you can physically rest, and your last words of wisdom can be shared. The inscription you write as your epitaph is your final message, a reminder of your legacy.

The sooner you write this message, the clearer your values will become in your life. And living up to your epitaph will give you a longer time to build your legacy.

Conclusion

My wish is that this book helps you see your greatest investment is in the people around you. Investing in your family starts with the basics of a good mindset.

The roles of parent and investor carry a great fiduciary responsibility. But this magic pairing makes some of the best-in-class humans I know and respect. They are people who understand value, how to nurture and grow assets, and how to pass them on to the next generation.

These two roles complement one another. Venturing down the career path as an investor made me a better parent. Learning how to be an engaged parent made me a great steward that nurtures my nest egg and wealth estate.

Being a great investor and a good parent are both areas that people can work on. It is easier to have both traits when they operate together. My perfect pairing is being an exceptional investor and good parent. While these two topics are usually discussed separately, with no clear connection between them, I hope this book brought them together for you in perfect alignment. Both endeavors entail great care, attention, deep value, consistency, and a long-term strategy that is greatly rewarded.

This book is just a start to the work an invested parent can do. I continue to sharpen my skills as an investor, but after market hours, I focus on my two greatest investments, my girls.

I still have much to learn as my young girls grow and mature, and as I continue to build relationships throughout my extended family. Hopefully, I'll be just as lucky with my family as I am with my financial investments and my coaching clients.

I also want to meet more mentors and older parents who can give me the advice and tools I need to grow as a father, just as my investing coaches did a few short years ago.

Everyone needs a coach, a helping hand, a teacher, or even just a guide to walk down the unfamiliar path with them. If you want to join with me on this path, then feel free to reach out to me with a complimentary 15-minute virtual visit to see if there is a right fit.

Those 15 minutes may save you 15 years of life's most humbling mistakes. Don't waste your life, grinding at the same 9-to-5 for far too long or grasping at every side-hustle and investment opportunity in the hopes of hitting the jackpot.

In the meantime, stay connected with me online at www.investedparenting.com

You will find links to my social media and free online videos that will help you become an invested parent.

From our family to yours, we pray that you are continually growing stronger together while leaving your own legacy of love, care, health and wealth.

About the Author

Alfred Gordon Liu is an investor, coach, and author from Vancouver, Canada. He's part of the great sandwich generation - one side is his two young girls, and the other side is his parents and in-laws. All three generations are strong and prospering in their best version of pandemic life. They often travel virtually all over the globe, hosting workshops and meetings.

Alfred combines investment strategies with best parenting techniques to help parents teach their children about family wealth while also coaching them how to invest in themselves!

He's endured all that life can throw at him with strength and resilience. His methods have been tested and forged by surviving three major economic crashes. Yet he never lost sight of what matters most in life, his family. Alfred spends his time paying it forward by teaching others how to invest using Rule1 Investing Strategies that he learned from his mentor Phil Town, Phil's daughter Danielle Town, and his family.

Alfred believes in empowering people to be their own best investors so they can live the life they want for themselves and their family by investing like the best parents in the world.

Alfred Gordon Liu

Learn more about Alfred Gordon Liu www.alfredgordonliu.com

You deserve more than just another parenting book or course on the internet! You need someone who understands what you're going through and can offer real-time guidance on how best to handle your situation.

If you are interested in customized coaching or other programs with Alfred's company, visit www.liucrown.com and book your first introductory session **FREE** on us.

Made in the USA
Middletown, DE
10 June 2021